	DATE DUE		

D1567510

WHOOPI GOLDBERG

OVERCOMING ADVERSITY

WHOOPI GOLDBERG

Ann Graham Gaines

Introduction by James Scott Brady,
Trustee, the Center to Prevent Handgun Violence
Vice Chairman, the Brain Injury Foundation

Chelsea House Publishers
Philadelphia

Frontis: Whoopi Goldberg displays her distinctive braids and sunny smile.

CHELSEA HOUSE PUBLISHERS

EDITOR IN CHIEF Stephen Reginald
PRODUCTION MANAGER Pamela Loos
MANAGING EDITOR James D. Gallagher
DIRECTOR OF PHOTOGRAPHY Judy L. Hasday
ART DIRECTOR Sara Davis
SENIOR PRODUCTION EDITOR Lisa Chippendale

Staff for **Whoopi Goldberg**
SENIOR EDITOR Therese De Angelis
ASSOCIATE ART DIRECTOR Takeshi Takahashi
DESIGNER 21st Century Publishing and Communications, Inc.
PICTURE RESEARCHER Patricia Burns
COVER ILLUSTRATION Matthew Rotunda
COVER DESIGN Keith Trego

First Printing

1 3 5 7 9 8 6 4 2

Library of Congress Cataloging-in-Publication Data

Gaines, Ann.
Whoopi Goldberg / by Ann Graham Gaines.
112 pp.   cm. — (Overcoming adversity)
Includes bibliographical references and index.
Summary: A biography of the single mother, former welfare recipient, and one-time drug addict whose determination helped her become a successful actress and television personality.
ISBN 0-7910-4938-8 (hc)
1. Goldberg, Whoopi, 1950—Juvenile literature. 2. Comedians—United States—Biography—Juvenile literature. 3. Afro-American comedians—United States—Biography—Juvenile literature. 4. Motion picture actors and actresses—United States—Biography—Juvenile literature. 5. Afro-American motion picture actors and actresses—United States—Biography—Juvenile literature. [1. Goldberg, Whoopi, 1950- . 2. Comedians. 3. Actors and actresses. 4. Afro-Americans—Biography. 5. Women—Biography.] I. Title. II. Series.
PN2287.G578G35 1998
791.43'028'092—dc21
[B]   98-41265
                                                              CIP
                                                               AC

CONTENTS

ON FACING ADVERSITY

James Scott Brady

I GUESS IT'S a long way from a Centralia, Illinois, train yard to the George Washington University Hospital Trauma Unit. My dad was a yardmaster for the old Chicago, Burlington & Quincy Railroad. As a child, I used to get to sit in the engineer's lap and imagine what it was like to drive that train. I guess I always have liked being in the "driver's seat."

Years later, however, my interest turned from driving trains to driving campaigns. In 1979, former Texas governor John Connally hired me as a press secretary in his campaign for the American presidency. We lost the Republican primary to a former Hollywood star named Ronald Reagan. But I managed to jump over to the Reagan campaign. When Reagan was elected in 1980, I was "sitting in the catbird seat," as humorist James Thurber would say—poised to be named presidential press secretary. I held that title throughout the eight years of the Reagan administration. But not without one terrible, extended interruption.

It happened barely two months after the Reagan administration took office. I never even heard the shots. On March 30, 1981, my life went blank in an instant. In an attempt to assassinate President Reagan, John Hinckley Jr. armed himself with a "Saturday night special"—a low-quality, $29 pistol—and shot wildly as our presidential entourage exited a Washington hotel. One of the exploding bullets struck me just above the left eye. It shattered into a couple dozen fragments, some of which penetrated my skull and entered my brain.

The next few months of my life were a nightmare of repeated surgery, broken contact with the outside world, and a variety of medical complications. More than once, I was very close to death.

The next few years were filled with frustrating struggles to function with a paralyzed right side, struggles to speak and communicate.

To people who face and defeat daunting obstacles, "ambition" is not becoming wealthy or famous or winning elections or awards. Words like "ambition" and "achievement" and "success" take on very different meanings. The objective is just to live, to wake up every morning. The goals are not lofty; they are very ordinary.

My own heroes are ordinary folks—but they accomplish extraordinary things because they try. My greatest hero is my wife, Sarah. She's accomplished a lot of things in life, but two stand out. The first has been the way she has cared for me and our son since I was shot. A tremendous tragedy and burden was dropped unexpectedly into her life, totally beyond her control and without justification. She could have given up; instead, she focused her energies on preserving our family and returning our lives to normal as much as possible. Week by week, month by month, year by year, she has not reached for the miraculous, just for the normal. Yet in focusing on the normal, she has helped accomplish the miraculous.

Her other most remarkable accomplishment, to me, has been spearheading the effort to keep guns out of the hands of criminals and children in America. Opponents call her a "gun grabber"; I call her a national hero. And I am not alone.

After a seven-year battle, during which Sarah and I worked tirelessly to educate the public about the need for stronger gun laws, the Brady Bill became law in 1993. It was a victory, achieved in the face of tremendous opposition, that now benefits all Americans. From the time the law took effect through fall 1997, background checks had stopped 173,000 criminals and other high-risk purchasers from buying handguns, and the law has helped to reduce illegal gun trafficking.

Sarah was not pursuing fame, or even recognition. She simply started at one point—when our son, Scott, found a loaded handgun on the seat of a pickup truck and, thinking it was a toy, pointed it at Sarah.

Fortunately, no one was hurt. But seeing a gun nearly bring a second tragedy upon our family, Sarah became determined to do whatever she could to prevent senseless death and injury from guns.

Some people think of Sarah as a powerful political force. To me, she's the person who so many times fed me and helped me dress during my long years of recovery.

Overcoming obstacles is part of life, not just for people who are challenged by disabilities, illnesses, or tragedies, but for all people. No matter what the obstacle—fear, disability, prejudice, grief, or a difficulty that isn't likely to "just go away"—we can all work to make this world a better place.

Director Steven Spielberg discusses a scene with novice actor Whoopi Goldberg on the set of The Color Purple *in 1984.*

1

A REALLY BIG BREAK

WHOOPI GOLDBERG WAS suddenly nervous. Four years earlier, while living in Berkeley, California, and working for a stage troupe known as the Blake Street Hawkeyes, she had developed *The Spook Show,* a one-woman stage performance in which she portrayed a variety of offbeat characters. While performing the show in New York at the Dance Theater Workshop in 1983, she was spotted by the well-known producer and director Mike Nichols, who offered to produce *The Spook Show* on Broadway. Renamed *Whoopi Goldberg: Direct from Broadway,* the show was a smash hit and was shown on cable television the following year. The record album of the Broadway show even won a Grammy Award for Best Comedy Recording.

But this was another matter. Steven Spielberg, the director of hugely successful films such as *Jaws, Jurassic Park,* and the Oscar-winning *Schindler's List,* had seen Goldberg's show while visiting New York. He had also heard that she was interested in his next project, a film adaptation of Alice Walker's novel *The Color Purple.* Spielberg had called Whoopi and asked whether she would perform her stage act for him and "a few friends."

So here she was in Los Angeles, in Spielberg's private screening room. But they were hardly alone. Spielberg had invited about 80 people to Whoopi's performance, including author Alice Walker and some of the biggest names in the American entertainment industry: singer Michael Jackson; film composer Quincy Jones, a coproducer of the movie and responsible for composing its soundtrack; and producers Jon Peters and Peter Guber, who owned the screen rights to the novel.

From the time Whoopi Goldberg was a child, she had held the firm belief that she could do anything she put her mind to. She had years of experience performing and improvising her act in front of audiences; she had stepped onstage for the first time more than 20 years earlier. She didn't mind "selling" herself in that way. All her life she had aggressively pursued what she wanted. Of her audition with Spielberg, she thought, "The worst I could do is stink."

Nevertheless, seeing 80 people crowded into the small screening room was a surprise, to say the least. But Whoopi recovered quickly and, with her usual aplomb, took the stage and blazed through her act. Working without a script, as she did on Broadway, she "created" a series of vastly different characters: a white "surfer girl" who has just learned that she is pregnant, a loudmouthed former drug addict who has a Ph.D., a physically disabled young woman who is getting married in two weeks, and a young black girl who wants to be blond. When members of the audience called out to Goldberg, she simply stayed in character and replied to them.

As soon as Whoopi came off the stage, Spielberg took her aside to tell her that her audition had been a complete success. He loved her work, as did Alice Walker and Quincy Jones. Her performance was not only funny, they said, but also touching. Goldberg's audience could easily empathize with the characters she portrayed.

Because Whoopi had little acting experience, she assumed that she would be cast in the minor role of Sofia. But Spielberg didn't want her for that part. Instead, he envisioned her as Celie herself, the heroine and main character in the novel.

Whoopi Goldberg was stunned. In the book *Whoopi Goldberg: Her Journey from Poverty to Megastardom,* James Robert Parish reports that she began to protest. "I was arguing with [Spielberg], saying, 'I don't want to play Celie. I don't want to mess you up if I'm not good,'" Whoopi recalled. "Then a little voice said, 'Goldberg, shut up. Take the gig, and if [you're bad], he'll fire you.' That's what we did," Whoopi said, "and it was great."

Playing Celie in *The Color Purple* would change Goldberg's life. She received $250,000 for her work in the movie—a vast amount of money at the time, and enough to guarantee her a measure of financial security that she had never had. Moreover, her performance gave her "star status" in Hollywood. She received an Academy Award nomination, which seemed likely to guarantee her a long and profitable film career.

In becoming a movie star, Whoopi Goldberg fulfilled a dream she had cherished since childhood. But it hadn't been easy for her to keep that dream alive. To achieve success, she had to overcome poverty, drug addiction, and the challenges of single motherhood. Today, Goldberg is close to her family, and her career is flourishing. She is active in many charitable organizations and contributes a great deal of her time and money to several causes. Recognized around the world for her trademark dreadlocks, broad smile, and outrageous personality, Whoopi Goldberg has emerged from years of hardship a spirited, determined, and outspoken woman.

Fulfilling a childhood fantasy: Goldberg grins impishly after a performance of her one-woman show at the Lyceum Theater on Broadway.

2

BORN TO PERFORM

CARYN ELAINE JOHNSON was born in New York City on November 13, 1955. At least 1955 seems to have been the year of her birth. Until the mid-1990s, Whoopi Goldberg routinely gave her birth year as 1949. Then she announced that she was actually born in 1955. She explained the discrepancy by saying that when she was first trying to make it as an actor, she wanted people to think she was older than she really was. "I lied about my age for a long time, because [otherwise] nobody would hire me to act," she said. "Everyone said I was too young. So, when I was twenty, I put six years on my life." Biographer James Robert Parish seems to have confirmed this by finding a New York City birth record that lists a "Caren" Johnson who was born on November 13, 1955. And Goldberg's first husband, Alvin Martin, says that he was born in 1952 and that Whoopi is three years younger than he is.

Caryn was the second child of Robert James Johnson and Emma Harris Johnson. Robert, born in 1930 in South Carolina, had headed north for New York City as a young man, where he worked at a number of jobs before he met and married Emma Harris. In 1949, the Johnsons had their first child, Clyde. By this time, however, their marriage was deteriorating, and Emma increasingly took over the responsibility of raising her child and earning steady wages. Shortly after their second child, Caryn, was born, Robert abandoned his family.

Emma Johnson never sought a divorce from her husband, nor did she reveal to her children the reasons why she and Robert parted. She has never discussed their relationship publicly; Goldberg says only that her mother has always been "pretty closemouthed" about the subject. As a result, Clyde and Caryn had little, if any, contact with Robert until the late 1980s, a few years before he died.

With her gift for embellishment, Whoopi Goldberg declares that her birth was a momentous occasion; she knew from her first moment of life that she was destined to be a performer. In her untitled book (generally referred to simply as *Book*), she says impishly:

> As soon as I popped into the birth room, I looked over in a corner, and there was my old man Destiny smilin' at me. My mother knew too. She felt I was gonna be special. Different. From the very beginning, she knew. The story she tells was that I came out—head-first, of course—pulled one arm through, looked around the delivery room, turned to the light, put my thumb in my mouth, and stared right back at all the folks who were staring at me. The spotlight was on me for the very first time, and I guess I thought it was kinda cool.

From the start, Whoopi says, she adopted a "don't mess with me" pose that amazed the doctors and nurses present at her birth. "They'd never seen a kid make such an entrance with such an attitude. They were coming in from all over, just to see," she jokes.

Towering high-rises in the Chelsea district of New York City, where Whoopi Goldberg grew up as Caryn Johnson. Goldberg fondly remembers the culturally rich and ethnically diverse neighborhood as a "microcosm of the world."

Despite her father's desertion while she was still an infant, Whoopi Goldberg remembers her childhood as happy. The Johnsons—Emma, Clyde, and Caryn— were a close family. Whoopi remembers feeling as though she were in a "partnership" with her mother and brother. She and her brother also spent time with their grandfather.

The Johnsons lived in a low-income housing project at 26th Street and 10th Avenue on the West Side of

Manhattan, in a neighborhood known as Chelsea. Today, the neighborhood is sadly decaying and plagued with crime, but it was a very different place during the 1950s and 1960s. Chelsea has a colorful history as a "melting pot" of races and ethnic backgrounds. While Caryn and her brother were growing up, the neighborhood's rich culture seemed to make up for the poverty in which most of the residents lived. "[I]t was a great microcosm of the world," Whoopi recalls. "We had people from Puerto Rico and Greece and Italy and Africa and Indonesia. . . . [We] had everybody."

"There was a real mix on our street," she says. "Every kid spoke ten lines of every language [because] you needed to be able to ask if so-and-so was home. Can I use the bathroom? Yes, I'll stay for dinner." Goldberg is quick to point out that Chelsea was a close-knit neighborhood, in which residents could walk safely to shops, church, and school. It hadn't yet become a rough place.

When fights occurred, they were organized "rumbles"—fistfights in which the participants made "appointments" to fight at specific times and places where no one else would be around. It may not have been the best way to solve disputes, Goldberg admits, but the method at least prevented innocent bystanders from the random injury and death that occur in today's drive-by shootings and other acts of urban violence.

Although she was often home alone while her mother worked, Caryn felt safe in her neighborhood. In the Chelsea-Clinton project where the Johnsons lived, a playground stood in the center of a cluster of apartment buildings. The neighborhood mothers would gather on a nearby park bench to watch over their children and others while they played. When she wasn't at work, Emma Johnson joined the group. This community effort kept kids in line. "We were always being watched," Whoopi remembers. "There was no escaping the eye of the neighborhood, and it was always incredible to me what these women picked up on. You knew the lady next door was gonna tell your mother if you had eight kids up in the apartment."

After Robert left, Emma Johnson had to work even harder to support her family. Although she had had ambitions of becoming a doctor, she was prevented from pursuing her dream by her inability to get a scholarship or afford the schooling needed for a degree. At the time it was also very difficult for women and African Americans to rise to this level in the field of medicine.

Instead, she became a nurse and worked at French Hospital. She would later become a teacher in a preschool program called Head Start, which was established by the federal government in the 1960s.

Even though Emma was often away at work, her children describe her as a wonderful parent who was determined to instill values and ideals in her children. She was loving but strict: "She could stop you from doing anything, through a closed door even, with a single look," Whoopi remembers, "that death-ray look that could melt concrete." But Emma also knew when it was wiser to give in. Whoopi likes to tell about the time when her mother sat her down in front of a plate of scrambled eggs that Whoopi refused to eat. Only days later, after sitting her daughter down in the same place every day, did Emma finally yield. She realized, Whoopi says, that a power struggle wouldn't improve her relationship with her child.

Whoopi also has fond memories of her brother, and she feels as close to him as she does to her mom. Clyde is six years older, so when they were children he left Caryn more or less on her own while he pursued his own interests. "[When] you're a kid, those six years are big," she wrote in *Book.* Nevertheless, Clyde always stood up for his kid sister. "[I]f somebody was bothering me, I could always tell Clyde," she says. "He backed me up, and I adored him. I still do."

Emma Johnson took care to establish family traditions for her children. In *Book,* Whoopi fondly recalls their Christmas celebrations. Every year, her mother brought home a tree, put it in a stand, and left it bare for a week or more. Then one night, she would join her children in decorating the tree and the entire apartment, until it looked like "a done-up department-store window." While Christmas carols played, they would string the tree with lights and hang tinsel and peppermint canes on its branches. They decorated the windows with spray cans of fake snow. And every Christmas Eve, they gathered around the black-and-white TV to watch *A Christmas Carol*—"The British version," says Whoopi, "the one with Alastair Sim." Today, Goldberg carries on her mother's Christmas traditions with her own family.

Whoopi Goldberg still remembers with delight the occasional excursions she and Clyde took with their mother whenever she had time and money. They went to the movies as often as they could, and sometimes they'd take the ferry to Liberty Island, where the Statue of Liberty stands. Caryn's favorite trips were to the popular amusement park at Coney Island in South Brooklyn. For these outings, Emma packed a huge picnic basket filled with foods that her children loved, such as fried chicken, Kool-Aid, and Ring-Dings. The three of them would ride the subway out of Manhattan to the park, where they spent the day picnicking, playing games of chance, and screaming with glee on the rides.

There were more simple joys as well. Back home, on summer evenings when the ice cream truck pulled onto their street, Emma tossed a quarter down from their

When money and time permitted, Emma Johnson took Caryn and Clyde on excursions to the popular Coney Island amusement park, shown here.

sixth-floor apartment window so that Caryn could buy herself a treat. Today, Whoopi Goldberg realizes that her family was poor when she was growing up. But she and Clyde didn't know it then, she says; they were happy, and they had what they needed.

When Caryn was six, her mother enrolled her in St. Columba's, a Catholic grade school near their apartment. Emma hoped that Caryn would get a better education there than at a public institution. But Caryn had difficulty in school almost from the start. Her teachers realized that she had great trouble learning new things, and before long they had convinced her that she was a "slow" child. They began to suggest to Emma Johnson that her daughter was mentally handicapped.

What Caryn Johnson's teachers didn't understand was that she was dyslexic. Dyslexia is a fairly common disorder that affects about 40 million American children and adults. Its most recognizable symptom is the reversal of letters, words, and numbers: "b" looks like "d" or "saw" looks like "was." Numbers such as 6 and 9 are mistaken for one another, and larger numbers, such as 72 and 27, are reversed by the dyslexic reader.

But dyslexia can also affect memory, handwriting, speech, and coordination. Dyslexics may have a hard time distinguishing right from left, tying shoelaces, or telling time. They may have trouble concentrating or have visual or speech problems.

Because of these many symptoms, dyslexics frequently have great difficulty learning what comes easily to nondyslexics, even though their level of intelligence is not affected. If undiagnosed, as in Caryn Johnson's case, the disorder sometimes leads teachers, other students, and even parents to believe that the dyslexic child is not very smart, or even mentally handicapped. As a result, that child may feel worthless, stupid, or incompetent.

Fortunately, dyslexia can be treated through special learning programs or therapy sessions that teach people how to recognize and control their disorder. Whoopi Goldberg, however, did not find out that she was dyslexic until she was an adult. Nevertheless, she feels fortunate that it was discovered at all. "I learned how to deal with dyslexia through a lot of hard work and the help of a lot of different people," she says. "If someone feels they have a problem with reading or learning, they should make someone aware of it. There's so much more knowledge about dyslexia now and they could get the help they need."

Caryn may have been a serious underachiever at school, and she certainly felt frustration over her learning difficulties, but she insists that none of that ever stopped her from pursuing her dreams. Emma Johnson taught her children that they could do or be anything. The world was theirs, she told them, as long as they were willing to work hard.

Goldberg was very young when she began to dream of being an actor. She spent hours watching movies on TV and in the local theater, sometimes sitting through three or four films in one day. She preferred films from the 1930s, 1940s, and 1950s, with stars like Bette Davis, John Garfield, Claudette Colbert, Clark Gable, and Carole Lombard. At the time, she didn't realize that the films she saw on TV were old or that some of the celebrities she watched were long dead. "I didn't even know these movies . . . were all in black and white," she said years later. "I figured they were in color—only to discover I was wrong when I [later] got a color TV."

Because Emma Johnson had instilled in her daughter the confidence to aim high, Caryn would imagine herself in the films she watched, especially the ones she saw in the movie theater with her mother. "I always thought of myself as the fantasy character with [the actors onscreen]," she recalls. "They didn't know I was there, but I could hear and see everything they were saying and doing. So I didn't have imaginary friends; I had [actor] John Garfield."

Emma Johnson also encouraged Caryn and Clyde to take advantage of the rich variety of cultural events that New York City had to offer. She supported Caryn's interest in the performing arts by sending her to the New York Philharmonic's "Young People's Concerts" conducted by Leonard Bernstein, and to Broadway shows such as *Joan of Arc,* starring Diana Sands; *The Great White Hope,* starring James Earl Jones; and *Hello, Dolly!,* starring Carol Channing.

Among the Broadway stage performances Whoopi Goldberg remembers seeing as a child is The Great White Hope, *which featured James Earl Jones (left) in the starring role of Jack Jefferson.*

Caryn's love of acting and a talent for mimicry served her well while she was growing up. At some point, she developed an ability to "double-talk," speaking proper English in a well-modulated voice at home, just as her mother had taught her and her brother, and using slang at school and on the streets so that she would sound more like her peers. When she playacted, she could make herself sound like anyone she wanted.

To Caryn, acting seemed like a natural thing to do. As a very young girl, she began performing at the Hudson Guild, a neighborhood community center that provided a number of educational programs for the residents of Chelsea. Caryn was instantly drawn to acting onstage. One of her teachers from St. Columba remembers that the Hudson Guild theater program "was Caryn's first love. Acting was in her genes. She was a performer. You couldn't miss it. She . . . played the lead in every play she was in."

Caryn Johnson was an energetic and outgoing kid, but she always felt that she was much different from the other children in Chelsea. Her love for the theater was unusual for a child of her age. While other kids "were all dancing to Motown," for example, she would be "singing a tune from *State Fair,*" a musical that premiered in 1945.

After attending St. Columba's, Caryn was enrolled at Washington Irving High, a public school just a few blocks from her home. But she lasted there only two weeks. Just after she started ninth grade, the 13-year-old dropped out of school. She would never return.

Whoopi Goldberg has given a number of reasons why she left school at such a young age. One is that she found school boring and uncreative. "You couldn't ask questions," she claims. "People would tell you what they thought you should know." But she's also said that her dyslexia prevented her from understanding many of the lessons she was supposed to learn. She was frustrated and discouraged by the attitude that most of her teachers displayed toward her. "I was [considered] retarded for a good part of [my childhood], according to all of the paperwork, and I just couldn't handle it," she says. More than anything else, she felt like a loner, a "weird kid" whose interests were too different from those of other kids for them to fully accept her. Even though many of her teachers remember her as outgoing and popular, Goldberg tells a different story. In a 1987 interview, she said:

> I was just not a popular girl. I couldn't get a boyfriend. I couldn't get into a clique. I felt I wasn't hip enough or smart enough or fast enough or funny enough or cute enough. I couldn't even dance well. The people who were those things were the people who were going places. . . . I wanted so much to be accepted that I'd hang out in the park with some of the girls and guys, and when they'd say, "Well, we want to get some candy," I'd run and I'd get some candy [for them]. But I'd come back and they'd have gone. And I'd sit and wait. What hurts so much about things like that is that I didn't learn. I'd get the candy again.

Goldberg did learn a lesson from such hurtful experiences, however. She says they taught her never to treat other people cruelly. "Sometimes, I get so busy, I get callous. I forget stuff," she admits. "But that memory has made me concerned about how I treat other people, because it's painful, still."

Once Caryn was out of school, Emma Johnson—who had fiercely fought her daughter's decision to drop out—urged her to at least find employment. Caryn did hold various jobs. For example, she served as a junior counselor at the Ethnic Culture Camp in Peekskill, New York. During this period, she continued to perform at the Hudson Guild, and she still attended concerts and visited museums. She even continued to ride out to the Coney Island amusement park. Caryn was also becoming involved in what she calls "hippie politics." As a teenager, she would hang out on the campus of Columbia University, where she joined in some of the student protests against the Vietnam War that were sweeping across American campuses. She

also marched in civil-rights demonstrations. But then she became involved with something that would threaten to ruin her life.

Before Caryn dropped out of school, she had experimented with marijuana and LSD, the fashionable drugs of the 1960s. Now, however, she began to use drugs much more heavily. In the late 1960s, illegal drug use was so widespread among young people that the practice seemed "almost normal" to them, in Caryn's words. In New York's Central Park, it was easy to simply join a circle of strangers who were passing around a joint. No one thought twice about it. No one discussed the consequences of heavy drug use. But Caryn also began to use harder drugs, such as acid, heroin, amphetamines, and barbiturates. "I did everything," she admits now. "And large quantities of everything."

A sign of the times: throngs of marchers protesting America's involvement in the Vietnam War parade down Fifth Avenue in New York City, April 1968. While still a teenager, Whoopi Goldberg became involved in antiwar student protests on the campus of Columbia University.

Today, Whoopi Goldberg refers to this period as her lost years. She stopped living with her mother, who was so deeply distressed by her daughter's drug abuse that she could not bring herself to discuss it with others. When Caryn left the housing project, she also dropped out of the Hudson Guild acting program. If she held any jobs during this period, there are no records of them. Don Sledge, a friend of the Johnsons' who worked at the Hudson Guild when Caryn began performing there, says that she seemed to simply vanish from her old life. "She was heard of from time to time," he says, "but she was gone from the community."

Caryn experimented not only with drugs, but also with sex. She had many sexual partners, but few—if any—steady or serious romantic relationships. At 14, a year after losing her virginity, she became pregnant.

At that time in her neighborhood, young unwed mothers were uncommon. She felt desperate and alone, ashamed of confiding in anyone about her situation—even her mother. So she tried to abort the pregnancy herself.

Using bits and pieces of folklore she'd heard from others, she drank a concoction of whiskey, bleach, rubbing alcohol, and baking soda. It made her violently ill, but she was still pregnant. Finally, feeling that she had no alternatives, she went to a public restroom near a park in Chelsea and used a wire hanger to abort the fetus—an extremely dangerous act that could very easily have cost Caryn her life.

Caryn started to bleed and felt excruciating pain. A week later, she had a regular menstrual period, to her great relief. But she has never forgotten the mental anguish, physical pain, and trauma of feeling completely alone. "I cry now sometimes when I think of it, when I think that I could have gone to my mother," she has said. She also is extremely thankful—and fortunate—that she did not do permanent physical damage to herself. "God

A young teen smoking marijuana at a rock festival in 1971. Goldberg recalls that her drug use ended because she became bored with it. Today, she is firmly against drug use. "There ain't no joy in a high— none," she has said. "[Drugs] ain't your friend."

was with me," she says today. "I punctured nothing. I didn't completely destroy my body," she has written, reflecting on how great a risk she had taken.

Often, teenagers can feel caught up in the here and now and forget past difficulties and the lessons learned from them. This was the case with Caryn, who became pregnant again a year later, when she was 15. Steeped in the late 1960s mentality of "free sex," Goldberg admits that she foolishly did not use contraceptives, even after her first pregnancy. She wasn't even sure where she could find birth control products. By this time, however, abortions had been legalized in the state of New York, and she went to a Planned Parenthood clinic. She also confided in her mother, who had grown increasingly concerned about her daughter's behavior, and with whom Caryn was now almost constantly at odds.

Eventually, Caryn realized that she had to stop her careless and self-absorbed ways. She was a drug addict; she had become pregnant more than once; she didn't have an education, a real home, or any goals. Her life was going to go nowhere unless she made a decision to change. When she was 17, Goldberg said years later, "My world started to get dark." She'd seen a number of friends overdose on drugs, and she began to realize that she too was in real danger of dying. But she also simply became bored with the drugs she was taking. "There ain't no joy in a high—*none,*" she declared in a 1991 interview. "You *think* there [is], because you feel good temporarily. But it feels good less and less often, so you've got to do it more and more often. It ain't your friend," she emphasizes.

Finally, in 1972, Caryn Johnson checked herself into Horizon House, a drug rehabilitation program in Manhattan. For four weeks, she endured a very strict regimen. She followed the House's schedule. She saw a counselor. She participated in group therapy. She completed assigned chores. And she left clean.

For some drug users, this kind of program is enough. Others, like Caryn, may have to kick their habits again and again. The process is very hard, Goldberg says. "I didn't stop altogether at once. It took many, many tries. You fall a lot because it's *hard.* But in the end it's worth it: you get your life back."

Today, Whoopi Goldberg campaigns against drug use of any kind. She describes her past drug use as reckless and stupid. And she rightly points out that illegal drugs today are far more potent—and dangerous—than those available in the 1960s. (Most marijuana in the 1990s, for example, is not only more powerful but also frequently laced with a variety of other drugs such as crack, PCP, or heroin. In some areas of the United States, it is even dipped in codeine cough syrup or embalming fluid.)

Don Sledge of the Hudson Guild remembers the change in Caryn Johnson after she "graduated" from Horizon House. She had become "mature, confident. She knew the ropes now. She knew what she wanted. She always knew where she wanted to go. She just had problems along the way."

Twelve-year-olds enrolled in a drug treatment program (left, seated at table) listen as a counselor speaks to other kids about treatment. As a teenager, Whoopi Goldberg checked herself into a similar program to end her drug problem.

Whoopi as a young actress.

3

ONTO THE STAGE

WHEN 17-YEAR-OLD CARYN JOHNSON left Horizon House, she vowed to change her life. Shortly after leaving the program, she began her first serious romantic relationship, with Alvin Martin, her 20-year-old drug counselor at Horizon House. Eventually, she moved out of her mother's apartment, where she had begun staying again, and into Martin's small apartment in the Greenwich Village section of the city.

The following year, in 1973, Caryn married Alvin Martin. Today, she says that one of the reasons she married was that she feared becoming "lost" again. She was eager to put her rootless years behind her but unsure of what would come next. She knew she wanted to pursue acting and needed a more stable life than the one she had been living.

Goldberg has also said that getting married seemed to her to be the inevitable next step in her life. "It seemed like the thing to do at the time," she says. "[Alvin] was bored with what he was doing and wanted to try something else. I figured nobody was ever going to marry me so I might as well do it just in case."

By the time they married, Alvin had left his job at Horizon House and was working as a bank clerk in Manhattan. He stressed that both of them needed steady jobs to get by financially, and he arranged for Caryn to get a clerical job with his company. Caryn hated the work. She had little patience with the formal environment of a large banking institution and the pressure to conform to dress codes and time schedules. Having kicked her drug habit and regained the ability to think clearly, Caryn began to remember the satisfaction that she'd found in acting and performing. She would have preferred to spend her time attending auditions and looking for acting gigs.

In May 1974, 18-year-old Caryn gave birth to a daughter, Alexandrea Martin. During Caryn's maternity leave from her job, the Martins moved to a better apartment in Manhattan, and later to a third one in Queens. But after Caryn's leave ended, she refused to return to work. Instead, she began taking small parts in off-Broadway plays, most of which paid nothing.

Now working two jobs and increasingly taking over the responsibility of caring for Alexandrea, Alvin found himself at odds with Caryn's dream of pursuing an acting career. The couple had begun to argue constantly about money and priorities. "She wanted to be a movie star, and I wanted to pay bills. The two things don't mix," Alvin Martin has said.

Within months of their daughter's birth and less than two years after they married, Caryn and Alvin split up. (They would formally divorce some years later, long after they had gone their separate ways.) With nowhere else to go, Caryn took her daughter to live with her mother. Once again, she was unsure of what she should do next.

She didn't have to wait long, however. About a month after moving back to Chelsea, Caryn got a call from a show business friend who was planning to drive to California and wanted company. Caryn readily agreed. In 1974, with Alexandrea in tow, she and her friend drove across the country, through Texas, to California in a "barf-green car." To Caryn's surprise, they ended up in San Diego, not Hollywood, as she'd imagined. But it was close enough to the "film capital" for Caryn.

Now in a strange city, far from the familiar surroundings of New York, Caryn was plagued with the fear that her decision had been too rash, that she had made a terrible mistake in moving to California. The pace there was much slower than she was accustomed to. She missed the excitement and commotion of Manhattan. And like many New Yorkers, she'd grown up without learning to drive, relying instead on the city's vast public transportation system to get around. In San Diego, it was different. People without cars had difficulty getting from one place to another. It would be a few years before Caryn saved enough money to buy her own car—a run-down used Volkswagen—and learned to drive.

The first thing Caryn needed to do was find a job to feed herself and her child. A high-school dropout, she lacked the education that could get her a well-paying job, so she took whatever she could find. She earned a beautician's license and ended up styling hair and applying makeup to corpses in a funeral parlor. (She would later joke that it wasn't so bad; it was quiet and the customers never complained.) She worked in a restaurant, as a bank teller, a bricklayer, and on several construction jobs.

No matter how hard she worked, though, she wasn't always able to make ends meet. At one point, a friend suggested that she think about going on welfare. Although it was a tough decision to make, Caryn realized that she had Alexandrea to think about. So she eventually accepted public assistance during the periods when she couldn't find work. And when she did get a job, she would dutifully report her income to the welfare department, which would deduct a portion from her next check. She was scrupulously honest, she says, because she never wanted her daughter to see her lying.

Unfortunately, some people unfairly stereotype those who are on welfare as lazy or incompetent. To this day, Whoopi Goldberg has never apologized for or denied accepting welfare. Although she acknowledges that America's public assistance program is sometimes abused, she maintains that "most folks on welfare would love to live decently, to feed, house, and educate their kids in a good environment. [But] the message is that there's work out there, when the truth is that there's not." The welfare system was meant to help people who fall on hard times, and in Goldberg's experience, most recipients strive to get back on their feet again as soon as possible to avoid being on welfare for long. For her, it was a cushion "not to rest my butt on, but to break the fall before I hit bottom."

Whenever she had time, Caryn Johnson auditioned for parts in local productions with repertory groups and dinner theaters. She even took a few gigs as a stand-up comic. But she encountered resistance from casting directors, not only because she still had little professional experience but also because she was black. At the time, most shows had all-white casts and were supported by white patrons, and many directors believed that their audiences were "not ready" for interracial plots. They would tell her that they were not interested in making such a "statement" in their productions.

Another reason Caryn had difficulty landing good roles was her unusual appearance. After she arrived in California, she began to cultivate her now-familiar hairstyle: a full head of long dreadlocks. She says that she adopted this look because it was comfortable and easy to care for, and she hopes that the "dread braids," plum-colored lipstick, and flat shoes or sneakers she sees many women wearing today have been influenced by her unique style.

Around this time, Caryn also decided to adopt a stage name. She figured that a more "gimmicky" name would help casting directors and audiences remember her. In a

1987 interview with *Playboy* magazine, Goldberg explained how she came up with her unusual name:

> The name was a fluke. A joke. It started when I was doing *A Christmas Carol* in San Diego. We'd sit backstage and talk about names we'd never give our children, like Pork Pie or Independence. . . . A woman said to me, "If I was your mother, I would have called you Whoopi, because when you're happy you make a sound like that practical joke whoopee cushion." It was like "Ha-ha-ha-ha—Whoopi!" So people actually started calling me Whoopi Cushion.

Emma Johnson was horrified. She told her daughter that she'd never be taken seriously as an actor with a name like that. Eventually, Caryn agreed to drop the last name, but she insisted on keeping "Whoopi." After years of inventing colorful stories about how she settled on "Goldberg," Whoopi admitted that her mother chose the surname and it

A young woman uses food stamps to purchase groceries for her family. Whoopi Goldberg, who was forced to go on welfare several times, believes that most welfare recipients prefer to support themselves instead of relying on government assistance.

just seemed to fit. Apparently, however, the Johnsons do have distant relatives with that last name.

Although Whoopi's friends and colleagues loved her new name, most reviewers did not. After one critic called it "ridiculous," Whoopi replied in a letter that it didn't really matter what her name was. Borrowing from William Shakespeare, she told him that a rose by any other name would still be an actor.

At home with her family and friends, however, Caryn Johnson still remains Caryn Johnson. She still views "Whoopi Goldberg" as a stage name, a persona that she assumes when she appears in public. For her, the distinction allows her and Alexandrea a measure of privacy.

Shortly after arriving in California, Whoopi joined the San Diego Repertory Theater, an organization formed in 1976 by two members of a street performance group called Indian Magique. The Repertory Theater presented avant-garde and experimental plays, first at San Diego City College and later in their own building, a former mortuary that became the Sixth Avenue Playhouse.

An adventurous group, the San Diego Repertory Theater had few of the reservations Whoopi Goldberg had encountered with other directors and theater organizations. She was welcomed without hesitation. She quickly learned that being a member of a predominantly white acting ensemble was both beneficial and challenging. With her dark skin and ethnic features, Goldberg stood out among her fellow actors and was easily recognized and remembered. But she also knew that, despite her talent, she would have to work twice as hard to get more than minor roles. Even in the accepting atmosphere of the San Diego Repertory Theater, her looks and her color prevented her from winning parts deemed appropriate only for white actors.

While Whoopi was working with the repertory group, she also put in time with an improvisational group called Spontaneous Combustion ("improv" actors make up their material as they perform, without using a script). Although

Whoopi Goldberg (shown here with Michael Richards of Seinfeld *fame) played five characters in the San Diego Repertory Theater's performance of Charles Dickens's* A Christmas Carol, *1977.*

she was learning a great deal as a member of the San Diego Repertory Theater, it was with Spontaneous Combustion that she acquired insight into human character and learned how to think fast on her feet while performing. Here she became friends with an actor and comedian named Don Victor. Before long, she had agreed to work as his partner, traveling the comedy circuit around San Diego and performing in popular venues like the Comedy Store.

At first, Victor and Goldberg worked for free. Later, however, they were paid a small fee for their performances. Their big break came in 1980 after Whoopi had attended a workshop given by a Berkeley, California, acting troupe called the Blake Street Hawkeyes. She invited members of the Hawkeyes to a performance of hers and Victor's. They were so impressed that they invited the duo to perform in

Goldberg in a 1981 production of Bertolt Brecht's Mother Courage. *Working in a repertory theater, where a group of actors play different parts in a series of productions, helped Goldberg expand her range and versatility.*

Berkeley. Goldberg and Victor enthusiastically accepted.

However, the day before they were to make the trip to Berkeley, Victor claimed illness and announced that he couldn't go. By some accounts, Victor was not ill but afflicted with stage fright, afraid of leaving the area where he was already recognized and accepted as an actor. Whatever the reason, Whoopi decided that she had no choice but to make the trip alone.

When David Schein, a member of the Hawkeyes, met Goldberg at the airport, she explained that she was there alone. He encouraged her to perform anyway. "Just do what you do when you work with Don and make the audience your partner," Schein counseled. Though terrified at the prospect,

Whoopi decided to take his advice. "Okay, I can do this," she told herself. "If it doesn't work, it doesn't work." To her surprise, her one-woman performance was a smash hit. An exultant Whoopi returned to San Diego feeling as though she had finally discovered her acting niche. "That [performance] was the birth of me as a solo character artist," she says.

In the meantime, Whoopi Goldberg was flourishing at the San Diego Repertory Theater. In 1977, she had played five separate characters in a stage performance of Charles Dickens's *A Christmas Carol.* In 1981, the year after her Berkeley debut, she landed the title role in the repertory theater's adaptation of *Mother Courage and Her Children,* a tragedy about a mother who loses three children to war. The play was written by German playwright Bertolt Brecht in 1939 and first performed and translated in 1941. In the San Diego Repertory Theater's version, the original German score was replaced by 19th-century American folk music, and the 17th-century peasant characters became blacks living during the American Civil War.

The play opened on June 11, 1981, and ran for a month. A review in the *San Diego Union* called some members of the cast "melodramatic" but praised Goldberg's performance. "The production does have a Mother Courage," the critic wrote. "The actor unfortunately called Whoopi Goldberg can play the part anywhere, so larger than life, so quick and deft physically and so infused with useful energy is she." A reviewer for the *La Jolla Light* declared that she had a "strong, immediate presence," and that she was "absolutely right for the part: playing each salty or ornery moment for all it's worth. Goldberg wipes virtually every other performer off the stage."

The aspiring actor known as Whoopi Goldberg had reached a turning point. Finally, she began see herself in a new light, as a solo character artist. Without hesitation, she began setting new career goals for herself and planning ways to achieve them. Her first decision was to move to Berkeley.

Goldberg as Celie in The Color Purple.

4

SUCCESS AND CONTROVERSY

SOON AFTER *MOTHER COURAGE* closed in July 1981 Whoopi Goldberg moved with Alexandrea, now seven, to Berkeley, a college town not far from San Francisco. Although she left the San Diego Repertory Theater group on very friendly terms, she had long been impressed with the Blake Street Hawkeyes and was eager to join them and try out her newly discovered talent as a character actor.

There was another reason Whoopi was moving. She had fallen in love with David Schein, the Hawkeyes member who had encouraged her to try her first solo performance in Berkeley the previous year. Whoopi and Alexandrea (called Alex) moved in with Schein. The single mother, who had often found herself leaving her daughter with friends or coworkers in San Diego while she pursued her career, now felt relieved that she could share parental responsibilities with someone else.

Even in the early 1980s, Berkeley remained an important center of an American "counterculture" that had originated in the 1960s during the country's involvement in the Vietnam War. Goldberg, who sometimes describes herself as a former hippie, found the town a pleasant and free-spirited place to live.

The Blake Street Hawkeyes proved a perfect fit for Goldberg. She constantly improvised with other members of the troupe in experimental plays such as *Token,* a play about the Great Plague of 17th-century London, or *Reverence for the Dead,* a musical featuring a character named Lee Harvey Ozball—an obvious spoof of Lee Harvey Oswald, who was arrested for assassinating President John F. Kennedy in 1963. At times, the Hawkeyes dispensed with the structured atmosphere of the theater and took to the streets to perform improvisational acts for appreciative passersby.

During this period, Whoopi Goldberg also began regularly performing her one-woman show in venues around Berkeley and San Francisco. At first she called the show *More Than One Person.* Later, she renamed it *The Whoopi Goldberg Show.* By October 1982, when she did a two-week run at the Blake Street Hawkeyes Theater, she had retitled it *The Spook Show,* explaining in the program note that the performance was dedicated to "all spooks living, dead, and yet to be born." The word "spook," however, also has a derogatory connotation as a slang term for an uneducated, stereotypical black person. For this reason many African Americans, who misunderstood Goldberg's intention of referring to a common human spirit, took offense at the name of her show.

The reviews for *The Spook Show,* however, were consistently good. Of Whoopi Goldberg's uncanny ability to "become" other characters while onstage, the *City Area Monthly* reviewer wrote that these characters were "created in such a way that they are separate people with histories of their own, a myriad of faces and situations that reach a wide-ranging audience." A critic for the *San Francisco Chronicle* declared that Goldberg

"displays a talent for sharp caricature and a sterling sense of comic timing. . . . She has an astounding ability to capture the gestures, inflections and speech pattern of a wide variety of types."

Whoopi elicited similar praise when she took her show on the road. "With no apparent script," the *San Diego Union* wrote, "she evolves each character vocally and visually before your eyes, and the results are fascinating." A *Los Angeles Times* critic called her "superb." In Calgary, Canada, she was hailed as "outrageously

"Fontaine," a bigmouthed former drug addict with a Ph.D. in literature, was one of the four main characters in Whoopi Goldberg's one-woman The Spook Show. *The performance was renamed* Whoopi Goldberg: Direct from Broadway *when it opened in New York in 1985.*

funny, but without ever sacrificing the humanity of her characters." Another critic praised her fearlessness during one performance when she came offstage to defuse a particularly unruly and hostile crowd.

As Whoopi Goldberg's reputation spread, the media began interviewing her. Whoopi was always careful to point out that her performance wasn't just for black or female audiences. She deliberately portrayed people of many different backgrounds, ages, and ethnic groups. Her aim, she stated, was not only to entertain but to anger people, to teach them about those who are different from them, and also to "give 'em a lot of love."

Whoopi has never abandoned that commitment. Throughout her career, she has resisted being assigned to a particular group in a way that separates that group from others. For example, she does not wish to be referred to as an African American. "It divides us as a nation and as a people," she explains. "It diminishes everything I've accomplished. . . . It means I'm not entitled to everything plain old Americans are entitled to."

Although Whoopi's years in Berkeley were mostly peaceful and happy, they were not without problems. Though her experience and reputation as an actor had grown significantly, she was still earning very little money. Even with the help of David Schein, she sometimes found it hard to make ends meet and was forced to accept public assistance more than once. By 1982, however, Goldberg was financially secure enough to go off welfare for good. "The *greatest* thing I ever was able to do was give a welfare check back," she remembers. "I brought it back to the welfare department and said, 'Here, I don't need this anymore.'"

Lack of money wasn't Goldberg's only problem during her years in Berkeley. She also seems to have struggled with drugs again. When one interviewer asked why Whoopi had turned down an offer to appear on a TV comedy show in the early 1980s, she said that part of the reason was her fear of having enough money to support a cocaine habit.

While involved with Schein, Whoopi also became pregnant twice and chose, with his support, to have abortions. Finally, at 26, having been unsuccessful with several birth control methods and absolutely convinced that she did not want more children, she had her Fallopian tubes tied. She was already finding it difficult to give Alex enough attention because of her career demands. In later years, she admitted that while she may have been a good friend to her preteen daughter, she was not as good a parent as she would have liked to be.

In 1983, Goldberg took her show, now called *Whoopi Goldberg Abroad,* overseas to Holland and Germany. Once back in the United States, she performed in San Diego, where people who had known her for years were amazed by how much her acting technique had improved.

By this time, Goldberg had also begun working on a very different kind of one-woman show, in which she portrayed Moms Mabley, the stage persona of a black comedian named Loretta Mary Aiken. Aiken got her start in New York in the 1920s, and by the 1940s she had become famous as Moms Mabley—an old, outspoken woman missing a few teeth and dressed in baggy, mismatched clothing and a floppy hat. The combination of Moms Mabley's motherly folk wisdom and her ribald delivery made Aiken so popular that in the 1960s she made several comedy records featuring her feisty character.

In her act, Whoopi Goldberg paid homage to Loretta Mary Aiken as a pioneer in the field of comedy. Her skill in accurately portraying Moms Mabley cemented Whoopi's reputation as a talented character actor. Once again, Goldberg began her run in Berkeley in October 1983 before taking her act on the road. She returned to Berkeley to close the run in May 1984. Goldberg

Loretta Mary Aiken, more popularly known as her fictional character, Moms Mabley. Whoopi Goldberg secured her reputation as a skilled character actor after portraying Moms Mabley in 1983 and 1984.

received stellar reviews, although a few critics declared that they wished to see more of the actor's own personality—an indication of just how popular Whoopi Goldberg had become.

In the midst of the *Moms Mabley* run, Whoopi received an exciting invitation. She was asked to perform *The Spook Show* in New York City at the Dance Theater Workshop on West 19th Street, just a few blocks from the apartment building where she had grown up.

Although audience turnout on the first few nights was poor, *The Spook Show* received an excellent review in the *New York Times* only a week after its premiere on January 27, 1984. Critic Mel Gussow called Whoopi Goldberg fresh and funny. "Despite the outrageous quality of much of her commentary," he wrote, "she averts bad taste and retains her winning personality."

After Gussow's review was published, the seats in the Dance Theater Workshop began filling up. Even celebrities showed up to see what the fuss was about. One night Mike Nichols, a renowned Broadway producer, attended Whoopi's show. Nichols remembers laughing so hard that he decided to go backstage afterward to meet Goldberg. By the time he saw her, though, he was crying over the show's poignancy.

Nichols's reaction was not unusual; many people who saw *The Spook Show* were struck by Goldberg's ability to show not only the humorous but also the dark and painful side of human life. But Whoopi Goldberg does not take complete credit for her portrayals of vastly different characters with the same human spirit. In a June 1987 interview, she described the process:

> I know I'm supposed to say I do a lot of work on these characters, but I don't. They kinda live in me. It's a residence hotel. They say things and express stuff that I would never express. . . . Whoopi disappears. I've learned that I have some control over them, but once the performance experience begins, there's not much I can do. I'm just the one who takes care of all the business. It will sound just as crazy as can be when people read this, but that's the way it is.

Mike Nichols presented Whoopi Goldberg with an amazing proposal: to produce her show on Broadway. But Whoopi wasn't quite ready for a big-time debut. Besides, she was committed to taking the show back to Los Angeles in March, and she was traveling to San Francisco to perform *Moms Mabley*. Before leaving the East Coast, however, she performed in a number of small, off-Broadway venues throughout New York City—including the Hudson Guild Theater, where she'd

Theater director Mike Nichols (center) was so impressed with Goldberg's ability to improvise onstage that he offered to produce her one-woman The Spook Show *on Broadway.*

gotten her earliest acting experience. There, Emma Johnson proudly attended every one of her daughter's performances.

In the meantime, Whoopi Goldberg was attracting a great deal of media attention. People across the country read about her in gossip journalist Liz Smith's column. On March 5, 1984, she was reviewed in *Newsweek* magazine. Comparing her to comedian Richard Pryor, the *Newsweek* critic declared that Goldberg "treads that treacherous territory that falls between stand-up comedy and legitimate theater."

Whoopi flew to Los Angeles five days later to open

The Spook Show, this time on a double bill with David Schein. Enthralled and delighted by the performance, top-notch comedians such as Robin Williams and Lily Tomlin befriended Goldberg and offered help and advice. Thanks in part to her well-known friends, she eventually signed with a respected talent management firm. "Just let her do what she wants," David Schein advised the talent agents handling Whoopi. "She's very surprising when she does what she wants." Whoopi Goldberg was well on her way to becoming a celebrity in her own right.

In the meantime, Mike Nichols had stayed in contact with Whoopi, hoping to persuade her to accept his offer of producing *The Spook Show* on Broadway. Finally, she consented and prepared to return to Manhattan. David Schein and Alex planned to stay in Berkeley so Alex wouldn't have to change schools. Whoopi felt a great deal of trepidation at being separated from Schein and her daughter. "I was tempted to say no," she recalled years later, "[because] I didn't know what it was going to do to my family. I knew they didn't want to come. If they had said, 'Don't go,' I would've been unhappy for a while, but I wouldn't have come." Instead, Whoopi and David decided to take Alex on a cross-country car trip to Vermont. There, they spent a few peaceful weeks on vacation before driving to New York City. After he dropped off Whoopi, Schein headed back to California with Alex.

Whoopi Goldberg fondly remembers the weeks of preparation for her Broadway debut. She felt great personal and professional respect for Mike Nichols, and she appreciated his efforts to promote and finance her show. Nichols worked hard to ensure that every aspect of the show ran smoothly, but the one thing he didn't try to control was Whoopi Goldberg herself. Although he watched her rehearse again and again, he let her decide what material to leave out and what avenues of thought to explore. Nichols was so "hands off" with Goldberg that she later regretted being headstrong and not seeking him out for advice more often.

Whoopi's show—renamed *Whoopi Goldberg: Direct from Broadway* to avoid controversy over the connotations of *The Spook Show*—debuted at the Lyceum Theater on October 24, 1984. The production ran for 150 performances, closing in March 1985. Goldberg received mixed reviews. Some criticized the producer for not insisting on more "mainstream" characters. Others claimed that although Goldberg's sketches were good, the show itself didn't have a central theme. "Whoopi Goldberg is reaching for something special in her act. She grasps it often enough to merit close attention," the *New York Times* said. One exceptionally critical reviewer called her a "three-legged horse," implying that her work was no better than a carnival sideshow.

But others proclaimed *Whoopi Goldberg* a huge success. Clive Barnes of the *New York Post* rightly predicted that the actor was bound to become a "cult hero" (in fact, many people returned again and again to see Goldberg's show; it became the "in" thing to do). The *Washington Post* characterized Whoopi's monologues as "flaky, funny, gritty, bizarre, and quite unexpectedly touching."

Around this time, Whoopi Goldberg began to experience another side of stardom. Photos of her appeared in tabloids under headlines that she was involved with whoever she might have been standing near in the picture—singer Paul Simon or actor Warren Beatty, for example. On a brighter note, HBO began airing an expanded performance of *Whoopi Goldberg* for cable TV viewers. The program proved so popular that in 1986 HBO began selling it as a home video.

The highest honor Whoopi Goldberg received was a Grammy Award for the recorded version of *Whoopi Goldberg: Direct from Broadway.* Although she wasn't nominated for

After the success of The Color Purple, *the newly popular Goldberg appeared on a number of television programs. Here she poses with her friend LeVar Burton during a 1993 appearance for the PBS series* Reading Rainbow, *which encourages children to explore the world through books. Burton displays Whoopi's children's book,* Alice, *which was published in 1991.*

a Tony Award, as some had expected, winning a Grammy made Whoopi dizzy with joy. She confided to one interviewer that she feared how easily fame could turn her into an egotistical person. What she loved about her newfound fame, she said, was that it allowed her to meet so many other creative people. The worst part of it was the hardcore business dealings and the seemingly endless phone conversations she was forced to conduct.

After her Broadway debut, Whoopi was suddenly in great demand. In November 1984 she was a guest on TV's popular late-night comedy show, *Saturday Night Live*. She also read for PBS-TV's *Reading Rainbow*. Some months later, in March 1985, she was among the celebrities invited to participate in ABC-TV's gala *Night of 100 Stars II*.

Even before she appeared on Broadway, however, Whoopi Goldberg had signed on with a project that seemed guaranteed to launch her into stardom. A few years earlier, she had read Alice Walker's Pulitzer Prize–winning novel *The Color Purple* (published in 1982). Walker had had a hard time finding a publisher for her novel, which was loosely based on her greatgrandmother's life. The story concerns an uneducated and oppressed black woman named Celie who was born in the Deep South during the early 20th century. While still a child, Celie is raped repeatedly by her stepfather, who then sells her two resulting children. He arranges for her to marry an equally abusive man whom she calls Mister. She is forcibly separated from her beloved younger sister, Nettie, who eventually travels to Africa as a missionary.

Though Celie writes religiously to Nettie, she never receives a reply, and she begins to believe that her sister has abandoned her. She doesn't know that Mister has hidden every letter Nettie has written back. Eventually, though, Celie meets her husband's mistress, Shug, a beautiful blues singer with a mind of her own. From

Shug, Celie learns to stand up for herself, and she takes command of her life. She leaves her husband and starts her own business.

Whoopi Goldberg was among the millions of fans who read Walker's bestselling book. She was so touched by the story that she wrote to Walker. If Walker were ever to consider selling movie rights to the novel, Whoopi told her, she would do anything to be involved in the film. "[I]f there's a movie," she wrote Walker, "I would very much like [to be involved in the project]. I'd be dirt on the floor. I'd do anything. And here's a list of references you can call just so you know I'm not a flake."

But Whoopi Goldberg needn't have introduced herself. Walker knew very well who Goldberg was; she had even seen her first show, and she wrote back to the actor and told her so. "I had seen her perform in a very small theater in San Francisco," the novelist recalls, "and during the show she came out and shook hands with members of the audience. I was one of them, and I knew that night she was magical."

Walker sent Goldberg's clippings and recommendations to Steven Spielberg, the director of hit movies such as *Jaws* (1975), *Raiders of the Lost Ark* (1981), and *E.T.: The Extra-Terrestrial* (1982). Spielberg had been chosen by executive producers Jon Peters and Peter Guber, and by Walker herself, to direct and produce a film version of *The Color Purple*.

Whoopi Goldberg heard nothing for some months. Then, while playing off-Broadway, she got a call from Spielberg, who asked her to come to Los Angeles to audition. She immediately accepted. In early 1985, after auditioning before the crowd of celebrities gathered in Spielberg's screening room, Whoopi Goldberg signed a contract with Warner Bros. to be paid $250,000 for performing the role of Celie in *The Color Purple*. Though this amount was not considered huge at the time, it was a windfall for Goldberg, who only three years earlier had been on welfare.

In agreeing to have her book made into a movie, Alice Walker had required not only that most of the cast be black but also that at least half of the behind-the-scenes crew be blacks, women, or ethnic minorities. But the nature of the film and the fact that the movie's producer-director was a white man would unleash a storm of controversy in the months before and after the film was released.

The Color Purple was filmed in eight weeks in the sweltering heat of Marshville, North Carolina. For Whoopi, it was a glorious time. Oprah Winfrey, who was at the time an up-and-coming Chicago talk-show host, had been "discovered" by Quincy Jones and was playing the role of Sofia. Goldberg and Winfrey quickly became friends. When Whoopi's mother came to visit, Alice Walker took the two of them out to dinner, along with several other women working on the movie.

Although Steven Spielberg is known as a detail-oriented director who carefully controls most aspects of his films, he and Goldberg nevertheless had a smooth working relationship. She felt comfortable telling him when she thought Celie might say or do something differently from the way he was asking her to perform. She even argued with Spielberg about the way makeup was applied to make her look as though she were aging.

The Color Purple was still in production when a group called the Coalition Against Black Exploitation began to protest the making of the movie. Assuming the movie would send the same "messages" the book had, the group's leader, an attorney named Legrand H. Clegg II, said that the book degraded black men and suggested that the average black family was dysfunctional. Clegg also protested Walker's description of Celie and Shug's physical relationship, saying that the author was "promoting" homosexuality. (The movie downplayed this aspect of the novel in an effort to appeal to a mainstream audience.)

When *The Color Purple* was released in 1985, early reviews were mixed. Some critics thought it was uneven.

Alice Walker, author of the Pulitzer Prize–winning novel The Color Purple.

Others, in complete opposition to the Coalition Against Black Exploitation, said that it diluted the powerful message of the novel—the individual's ability to triumph over oppression. On the other hand, noted film critics such as Gene Shalit loved the movie. Shalit described it as a "great, warm, hard, unforgiving, triumphant movie." He continued, "There is not a scene that does not shine with the love of the people who made it." Nearly all critics praised the movie's cinematography and musical score, and the cast—especially Whoopi Goldberg—received very favorable reviews.

The *New York Times* declared that Goldberg had "outacted" every other actor in the film. The *Los Angeles Times* agreed, describing Whoopi Goldberg's "slow, incandescent smile" and her portrayal of Celie's growth as "stop-motion flower photography." The *Hollywood Reporter* declared that Goldberg's depiction of Celie's "emergence from slavery to radiant womanhood is a joy to behold."

The Color Purple grossed $80 million at the box office and received 11 Academy Award nominations, including Best Picture and Best Actress of 1985. But the controversy over the movie didn't let up. Members of the National Association for the Advancement of Colored People (NAACP) picketed theaters where the movie was showing, protesting that it portrayed black Americans in a very poor light. Whoopi Goldberg disagreed with the protesters. The movie, she insisted, was more than a story about African Americans. "It's not about blacks," she said. "It's not even about sexism. It's about a search of self. Celie has no idea that to be kissed you don't also have to be hit. Just look into my eyes. I know what I'm talking about. I've been around the block a few times."

Goldberg also feared that the protests over *The Color Purple* would discourage filmmakers from taking on other "black" projects. When Goldberg—ironically—was named Entertainer of the Year by the NAACP in 1990, she made sure to mention the organization's reaction to her first film. She hoped, she said, that in their naming her and in her accepting their award, both she and the members of the NAACP had "grown up."

Whoopi Goldberg did not win an Academy Award, but she hadn't really expected to. "I was probably lucky not to win," she later said. "If I had, there'd have been nowhere for me to go. . . . Now [people] will wait for me to get better." After all, her work had earned her

a nomination, and she now had a successful Broadway show to her credit. She had finally become a bona fide celebrity.

The actress was not about to rest easy, however. She was eager to find more film roles to add to her growing list of accomplishments. But she believed that the toughest part of her climb to success was behind her. She did not realize how many struggles still lay ahead.

Goldberg received high praise for her portrayal of Celie in the film The Color Purple. *"She can, by reacting, out-act everybody else on the screen," one critic enthused.*

In addition to acting, Whoopi is also dedicated to promoting a number of charitable organizations. Among the most prominent are the Comic Relief *HBO specials, which benefit America's homeless. Here Goldberg poses with fellow emcees Billy Crystal (left) and Robin Williams (right) for* Comic Relief V, *which aired in 1992.*

5

TRIAL AND ERROR

DESPITE HER GREAT SUCCESS in *The Color Purple,* Whoopi Goldberg found herself at loose ends in the years immediately following the movie's release. Before landing the part of Celie, she had imagined herself pursuing a career as a character actor in films. Once she received an Oscar nomination, however, that goal seemed too limited. She believed that her screen debut in *The Color Purple* would convince other film executives and producers that she had the talent to undertake major film roles.

But Goldberg had the weight of tradition to contend with. Even in the 1980s, a black actor rarely landed a starring role in a major motion picture. Throughout the history of Hollywood's film industry, only a few African Americans enjoyed success on-screen, and they were nearly always relegated to a limited range of roles. Between 1929 and 1935, for example, the black actor known as Stepin Fetchit appeared in 26 films—always as a slow-witted servant to whites. Bill "Bojangles" Robinson, who appeared in several movies during the 1930s, served as a foil to white child-star Shirley Temple.

The 1940s were not much better for African-American performers. Actors such as Lena Horne, the Nicholas Brothers, and Dooley Wilson were typically used as "specialty" acts in musical sequences that could easily be edited from film copies distributed in the Deep South. Although in the 1950s a number of black actors, such as Sammy Davis Jr., Harry Belafonte, Diahann Carroll, Eartha Kitt, and Sidney Poitier, were offered more promising roles, they were still limited by filmmakers who had no desire to be pioneers in breaking the industry's color barrier. Only Poitier landed mainstream roles: in 1963, he became the second black actor ever to win an Academy Award, for his lead role in *Lilies of the Field.* (Hattie McDaniel, who appeared in the classic film *Gone with the Wind,* received an Oscar for her 1939 performance.)

In the early 1970s, when Whoopi Goldberg was a teenager, a series of films featuring black lead characters became box-office hits. One of the characters was a promiscuous private eye played by Richard Roundtree in the movies *Shaft, Shaft's Big Score!,* and *Shaft in Africa.* Another was a Harlem drug dealer who was featured in the films *Superfly, Superfly T.N.T.,* and *The Return of Superfly.* These movies, intended to appeal to African-American audiences, are now often called "blaxploitation" films because of their stereotyped characterizations of black men. They did little to promote a realistic portrait of the average African American.

When Whoopi Goldberg began her film career, only two other black actors, Richard Pryor and Eddie Murphy, could be categorized as movie stars. Pryor eventually dropped out of filmmaking—first because of serious burns he sustained in a suicide attempt, and later when he was stricken with multiple sclerosis. Eddie Murphy, on the other hand, became a major film actor, riding high on the success of the 1984 movie *Beverly Hills Cop.*

After *The Color Purple,* Whoopi was surprised to discover that few filmmakers seemed interested in her work. So she decided that instead of waiting for film

roles to come to her, she was actively going to seek them out. Whoopi believed that the common perception among movie producers that audiences preferred whites in starring roles was simply wrong. Those who thought that way, she maintained, were underestimating the intelligence of their audience.

But Goldberg received few positive responses during her search for bigger movie roles. For example, when she heard that Rob Reiner was casting a movie called *The Princess Bride,* a comic adventure tale set in medieval times, she phoned Reiner. Under the guise of a casting agent, she proposed that he consider Whoopi Goldberg for the title role. Reiner cut her off. He assumed that she was making what he considered a bad

Sidney Poitier with actress Lilia Skala in Lilies of the Field *(1963). Poitier was one of the first black actors to break the "color barrier" of the film industry; he received an Academy Award for his performance in this film.*

joke. Other movie executives advised Goldberg to try to conform to what they considered conventional beauty standards. Get rid of the dreadlocks, they'd say, or wear more makeup and dress differently.

One day, however, she got a call from producers Lawrence Gordon and Joel Silver, who were about to start work on a new romantic comedy-thriller. They had originally given the lead female role—a computer programmer named Terry Doolittle who helps rescue a British spy—to Shelley Long (who had played Diane Chambers in the TV sitcom *Cheers*). But when Long dropped out of the project, they called Whoopi Goldberg.

Delighted, Whoopi believed that she finally had the opportunity to display her acting versatility. Unfortunately, once she signed on, the producers decided that the movie would no longer work as a romantic comedy. Instead, they had writers retool the script so that Goldberg's character would only feel a romantic attachment from afar; there would be no onscreen love scenes. "They were trying to be so careful not to point [the character] up as being black. . . . [T]hey made her so bland that she was boring," Whoopi recalled. "And I said . . . 'I could fall in love just as quick as Shelley Long could.'"

Whoopi later recalled with some bitterness that the producers had behaved as though someone like her couldn't possibly carry a love scene. In doing so, they had belittled her acting ability. Moreover, she claimed that although she had been told she would have a great deal of input into her character, in the end she had very little creative control.

The amended film, called *Jumpin' Jack Flash,* hit movie theaters in 1986. Although it featured a number of promising comic actors in addition to Goldberg, including Annie Potts, Jon Lovitz, Phil Hartman, Tracey Ullman, and Jim Belushi, the movie was panned by most critics. The *Village Voice* declared that the movie "wallows in the predictable. Whoopi's shtick is always

Goldberg as computer operator Terry Doolittle, who receives mysterious messages from an undercover agent in Jumpin' Jack Flash.

played against targets big as elephants: wealthy people, British aristocrats, police, bank managers." But once again, Whoopi Goldberg herself was favorably reviewed. Many critics thought that her talent was far better than the poorly written script. "She makes *Jumpin' Jack Flash* seem a lot hipper than it really is," the *Los Angeles Times* said. "[If the film] proves anything, it's that its star . . . is an absolute movie natural: She can shine in the most ragged circumstances."

Despite Whoopi's frustration over her stagnant movie career, 1986 was a good year for her professionally. In March, she became the first black woman to be named Female Star of the Year at the prestigious ShoWest industry trade convention in Las Vegas. That year, she also became involved in what has become a long-term fund-raising commitment. An important producer and screenwriter named Bob Zmuda, who had organized previous charity events, was interested in gathering together a group of stand-up comedians to appear in a fund-raiser to benefit the homeless. Robin Williams, Billy Crystal, and Whoopi Goldberg were among the first volunteers.

The three comedians threw themselves into the new project with great enthusiasm. As part of their preparation, they read widely about the problem of homelessness in America. They also visited shelters in the Los Angeles area and spoke with some of the homeless. Goldberg remembers one man telling Billy Crystal to "tell them we're *not* all bums." They also traveled to Washington, D.C., and to New York City, where they held press conferences to draw attention to the fund-raiser.

On March 29, 1986, *Comic Relief* opened to a sold-out audience at the Universal Amphitheater in Los Angeles. Dressed in matching tuxedos, Goldberg, Williams, and Crystal acted as emcees for a program that featured well-known performers such as Steve Allen, George Carlin, Dick Gregory, Michael J. Fox, Bob Hope, Jerry Lewis, Weird Al Yankovic, and Henny Youngman.

Comic Relief ultimately raised $2 million for the National Health Care for the Homeless Program. Under an agreement with HBO, it aired as a cable network special, and portions of it were later released as a home video. Originally conceived as a one-time event, the fund-raiser was such a smashing success that it became a yearly commitment for all three comedians. Goldberg's appearance made it clear to her audience that she was a dedicated fundraiser, determined to stay involved in worthwhile causes.

During this period, Whoopi did make a number of films, but most of them were forgettable: *Burglar* and *Fatal Beauty* (1987), *Clara's Heart* (1988), and a made-for-TV movie, *Kiss Shot* (1989). She also had a cameo in *Beverly Hills Brats* (1989). In 1988, she starred in a rather unconventional one-character movie called *The Telephone,* in which she played a depressed actress who holed up in her apartment, making contact with the outside world only by telephone. The result was a disaster. Before the movie was released, she sued New World Pictures and director Rip Torn, claiming that they had violated her contract by planning to release a different version of the film from the one she had approved (she lost the suit less than two months later).

Although Whoopi Goldberg remained unsatisfied with her film career during the 1980s, she did frequently appear on television, making guest appearances in several sitcoms, such as *Moonlighting,* starring Cybill Shepherd and Bruce Willis. She also performed in TV specials with comedians like Carol Burnett. HBO even signed her up for her own special, *Whoopi Goldberg's Fontaine: Why Am I Straight?,* an edited version of her performance at the Mayfair Theater in Santa Monica, California. In 1987 she also cohosted a program called *Scared Straight: Ten Years Later.* And she landed a recurring role on *Star Trek: The Next Generation,* a TV show with a big cult following.

Goldberg also returned to the stage with a one-woman show she called *Living on the Edge of Chaos,* featuring a new array of original characters. But though she became known in the industry as a workaholic, her lack of success in films led the press in 1989 to label her a "flash in the pan" and a "has-been."

In her personal life, Goldberg was experiencing changes as well. Even before her success in *The Color Purple*, her relationship with David Schein had begun to unravel. In a 1985 interview with *People* magazine, which had named Goldberg one of the 25 most intriguing people of the year, she said that their troubles had begun when she traveled to New York to perform *Whoopi Goldberg: Direct from Broadway*. Just as she had feared at the time, the distance put a great strain on their relationship. Eventually, Schein relocated to Chicago, Illinois.

In 1986, Whoopi began dating a Dutch filmmaker named David Claessen. The two shared a number of professional interests, and their relationship blossomed. On September 1, 1986, Goldberg and Claessen got married at a small chapel in Las Vegas, Nevada. The following week, Goldberg's manager threw a huge wedding reception for the newlyweds. The guest list included celebrities such as Cher, Dolly Parton, Barry Manilow, and Robin Williams. Goldberg and Claessen then flew to Europe for a six-week honeymoon.

But the marriage was brief. In May 1988, Whoopi Goldberg claimed in an interview that Claessen had only married her "to further his career as a filmmaker." Five months later, she filed for divorce. She would later claim that the relationship had been so bad that it left a "permanent scar," and that Claessen had put her in debt.

During her marriage to Claessen, Whoopi's relationship with her daughter, Alex, now a teenager, also became strained. Alex no longer lived full-time with Whoopi, who had moved to Los Angeles to make movies. Emma Johnson had relocated to Berkeley, and Alex chose to stay there with her grandmother, where she could attend a familiar school and be near her friends. Unfortunately, Goldberg

was so caught up in her own professional and personal life that she found little time to spend with Alex, and mother and child began to drift apart.

In 1989, Alex, now 15, called her mother, who was on location on a movie shoot, to tell her that she was pregnant. She did not wish to marry the baby's father, she insisted, and she intended to keep the child.

Whoopi was stunned. She knew firsthand what it was like to try to raise a child while still very young. Nevertheless, after the initial shock, she supported her daughter's decisions. She was proud of Alex for feeling confident enough about her situation to tell her mother the truth. She also realized that Alex may have been unconsciously trying to find a replacement for the motherly love and support she had sought but never received from Whoopi.

Although Whoopi Goldberg's busy film career put a strain on her relationship with her daughter, Alex, the two women, shown here attending the 1991 Academy Awards ceremony, are now close.

Years later, Whoopi Goldberg reflected on the mistakes she had made with her daughter:

> You make specific choices with children. I didn't make the mother's choice. I chose my career. I should have cared more. I was selfish, and I am selfish. But I just felt that when opportunities came up, I had to take the ball and run. I would have become very angry and bitter otherwise. I've learned since what being a mother means, what those responsibilities entail. I know that I have to care more.

Whether or not Whoopi Goldberg had let her daughter down, her own fame caused the difficult situation to be trumpeted in newspapers, magazines, radio talk shows, and TV programs. Many blamed Whoopi for being an unfit mother who had allowed her daughter to grow up without discipline or support. Others questioned Alex's morality. The very public discussions of what should have been a private family matter irritated and upset Goldberg. "I got a lot of angry letters from people when my granddaughter was born, because Alexandrea was a young single mother," Whoopi said. She went on:

> [They said] "You go around telling kids about birth control and safe sex, and your own daughter does not follow the advice." She didn't. I know now because she wanted a baby. . . . My daughter got pregnant because she did not feel that singularly she was enough. Is it other people's business? I don't know. What people were criticizing is that they thought money was going to prevent her from getting pregnant, or fame would do it.

Whoopi concluded that although her daughter may have made a decision that she didn't agree with, it was Whoopi's responsibility to support her.

Despite the media attention, Alex enjoyed her pregnancy. "She was one of those women who floated around [she was so happy to be pregnant]," her mother recalls. On November 13, 1989—Whoopi's 34th birthday—she became a grandmother to a baby girl named Amarah Skye. After Alex married in 1993, she gave birth to another child, whom she named Jerzey.

Goldberg loves to talk about her grandchildren, and the bond of motherhood seems to have strengthened her relationship with her daughter. Goldberg plays a strong role in her grandchildren's lives, in a way that she hadn't with her own daughter.

At the same time, Whoopi still felt stalled in her professional life. One issue that bothered her greatly was that filmmakers were hesitant to consider her because of her unconventional physical appearance. "I've taken so much heat about my hair and the way I look," she said during this period. "Well, this is it. And I'm not going to try and change myself because other people are uncomfortable with me. I'm comfortable with me. . . . So why should I be uncomfortable to make other people feel better? That's not a good idea to me."

Goldberg pointed out that she also had trouble finding producers who would cast her in movies intended for black audiences. When film director Spike Lee criticized Goldberg for accepting roles in "white" movies that he felt were undignified or exploitive, she lashed out at him. Why hadn't Lee or other black directors like John Singleton ever asked her to appear in their films? she demanded. Nor was she offered starring roles opposite African-American stars like Denzel Washington.

Finally in 1989, Whoopi Goldberg received two breaks. In March, CBS announced that she would costar with Jean Stapleton (of *Archie Bunker* fame) in a sitcom called *Bagdad Café.* The series was canceled in less than two years, but it buoyed Goldberg's spirits for a time.

That same year, Whoopi landed a role as a maid named Odessa Cotter in the movie *The Long Walk Home,* a story about the yearlong 1956 boycott that helped end segregation on buses in Montgomery, Alabama. The movie focuses on the ways in which Cotter and her wealthy white employer, Miriam Thompson (Sissy Spacek), react to the boycott.

To prepare for the role, Goldberg traveled to Alabama to speak with several women who had lived through that turbulent period of American history. She traveled the long routes they took on their way home from jobs as maids, from posh white neighborhoods to their own, poorer sections at the other end of the city.

Playing this role was an eye-opening experience for Whoopi Goldberg. For the first time, she says, she understood what was at stake for African Americans who fought for civil rights. "I went down there . . . with

Whoopi Goldberg and Jean Stapleton on the set of the short-lived TV series Bagdad Café.

a little bit of an attitude . . . kind of like, 'Well, what took you all so long,'" Whoopi said. She soon learned from the women with whom she spoke that their acts of rebellion had been far from simple. "You did not buck the system," they told her. "You know, we continued to take care of business. We showed them that in fact one person who finds another person who finds another person can make a difference. We did not write ourselves off." Goldberg added, "You have to understand that we're talking about 1955, and the bottom line was you didn't sass or talk back or they killed you. Very simple. You died, or you lost your job."

These stark facts made the actress even more aware of how much work would go into preparing for her part.

Goldberg and Lexi Faith Randall in The Long Walk Home. *To prepare for her role, Whoopi spent time with some of the women who had lived through the 1956 bus boycott in Montgomery, Alabama. "I understand now what these people had to deal with," she said after filming was completed.*

"I couldn't even give [Odessa Cotter] a nineties look. . . . I had to just . . . sit on it," she said, describing how she had to dispense with her usual flamboyance and improvisation. As a result, "people kept saying [that] there was . . . this quiet strength [in my performance]." But that wasn't what Goldberg was feeling. "It's this rage," she said. "It's not a quiet strength. It's this silent rage. . . . I understand now what these people had to deal with, because there was nothing they could do."

The release of *The Long Walk Home* was delayed so that it would not coincide with that of a similar film, *Driving Miss Daisy,* in which Morgan Freeman plays the chauffeur for a wealthy white woman (Jessica

Tandy) during the same time period. Perhaps because of its similarity to the highly successful *Driving Miss Daisy,* the box-office figures for *The Long Walk Home* were ultimately disappointing. Goldberg herself came under fire from some African Americans, who criticized her for accepting a role that seemed to stereotype blacks as subservient to whites.

Despite the criticism, however, Goldberg received the NAACP Image Award for her role, and reviewers were generous. One critic described her as "the movie's surprise, for she turns out to be ideal in the role of a woman whose character is the antithesis of everything implied by the name Whoopi. She underplays the anger that inspires her to walk ten miles to work, and she underplays the weariness too. [Her] performance holds the movie together."

A few months before Whoopi Goldberg began film-ing *The Long Walk Home,* she had heard from a former colleague, Barry Josephson, who was looking for actors for a new film called *Ghost,* produced by Paramount Pictures. After reading the script, Josephson said, he had immediately thought of Goldberg to play the part of Oda Mae Brown, a scam artist pretending to be a psychic who discovers that she really does have supernatural powers. Whoopi was immediately interested, and she began to campaign for the part. It would turn out to be the most rewarding role in her film career.

A jubilant Whoopi Goldberg after winning an Oscar for Best Supporting Actress for her role in the 1990 film Ghost.

6

HIGHS AND LOWS

THE PART OF ODA MAE BROWN in *Ghost* may have been a supporting role, but it was a choice one. Whoopi Goldberg quickly contacted the director of the film, Jerry Zucker, and offered herself for the role. She auditioned early in the casting process, but Zucker turned her down. He was looking for an "unknown," an actress who did not have the name recognition that Whoopi Goldberg had already earned. "I didn't want the role to be a vehicle for anybody," Zucker said later.

The director also thought that Whoopi was just a bit too "zany" for the part. Once again, her distinctive acting style made her difficult to place in a mainstream film. Zucker wasn't sure that she would be the right person to carry Oda Mae's dramatic scenes in the film. So he kept auditioning other actresses. "They woke folks up from the dead to talk about that part," Goldberg joked. Finally, with prodding from Patrick Swayze, who would be playing the role of Sam Wheat in the film and who was a big fan of Whoopi's, Zucker took a second look at Goldberg and decided to sign her on. Filming began in July 1989.

The plot of *Ghost* revolves around a live-in couple, a New York banker named Sam Wheat (Swayze) and a sculptor, Molly Jensen (Demi Moore). While on their way home from the theater one night, they are attacked and Sam is murdered by a mugger. His spirit remains on earth, however, because it has unfinished business. Sam needs to tell Molly that his death was not the result of a random act of violence, but a planned murder by a so-called friend of theirs. Now her life is also in danger. In search of a way to warn Molly, he uses the services of Oda Mae Brown (Goldberg), who advertises herself as a psychic.

But Oda Mae is a con artist who only pretends to contact deceased loved ones. With Sam's coaching, however, she convinces Molly that Sam is really trying to reach her. In the course of the movie, Oda Mae discovers that she truly does have psychic powers.

Whoopi Goldberg greatly enjoyed filming *Ghost.* She got along well with Zucker and had great respect for the acting abilities of Swayze and Moore. The hardest part, she recalls, was trying to interact with what was supposed to be a ghost figure. In the early scenes of the movie, before Oda Mae knows what's happening, she can't see Sam Wheat, so Goldberg had to pretend that she couldn't see Swayze either. "It [wasn't] easy," Whoopi recalls. "Every once in a while we would be doing a scene and everything would seem to be going okay when suddenly Jerry [Zucker] would call cut. I would ask him what the problem was, and he would tell me I was looking at Patrick. . . . So we would shoot the scene again and I would be looking all around and trying not to look at Patrick."

Ghost was the surprise hit of the summer of 1990, grossing $218 million in less than a year. By the time it was released on videotape in March 1991, pre-orders had reached nearly 600,000, making it the biggest

rental title ever. The movie's soundtrack album, which featured the Righteous Brothers' recording of an old tune called "Unchained Melody," sold more than 500,000 copies.

Audiences clearly loved *Ghost,* and most reviewers, though unimpressed with the overly sentimental nature of the story, also had favorable comments. The *Los Angeles Times* critic Sheila Benson wrote, "In our increasingly fragile and unpredictable world, *Ghost . . .* might well strike a seductive chord." She praised Whoopi

Oda Mae Brown (Goldberg) speaks to the ghost of Sam Wheat (Patrick Swayze) in the film Ghost. *Trying to play her role against a character who was supposed to be invisible was a stretch for the actress. "Have you ever tried to work with somebody who is there but not there?" Whoopi asks. "[It] was very hard and sort of crazy-making."*

Goldberg wholeheartedly: "Oda Mae . . . is Goldberg in her element, giving the film its kick and energy. In the three-way scenes with Sam and Molly . . . Goldberg is gleefully, wickedly funny. Working out the villain's comeuppance she's even better." *New York Times* critic Janet Maslin said Goldberg turned in a better performance in the movie than either Swayze or Moore: "This is one of those rare occasions on which the uncategorizable Ms. Goldberg has found a film role that really suits her, and she makes the most of it."

In February 1991, Whoopi Goldberg received her second Academy Award nomination, this time for Best Performance by an Actress in a Supporting Role. Dressed in a full-length black sequined gown, she attended the Oscar ceremony with her daughter, Alexandrea.

Although Goldberg had been practicing all her life for the moment when she might stand onstage and receive an Academy Award, she was overwhelmed when the presenter, Denzel Washington, announced her name. At first, she was so stunned that she almost didn't stand up to receive the award. "I was still sure that Denzel was going to go, 'Oh, no, no, I—that's what I was thinking, but here's the real winner,'" she recalled. Once she was standing behind the podium with the Oscar in her hands, Whoopi found herself speechless. Later, in an interview with *Parade* magazine, she explained her feelings:

> When I finally got the opportunity to give the speech I'd been practicing for years, I didn't have it. I was so floored, there was nothing I could do except sort of gasp, "Thank you." I looked around and saw all those people sitting there—Sophia Loren, Gregory Peck. And then I just wanted to say "thank you" to them for being in all those movies I got to watch. For letting me come and play.

Winning an Oscar is usually a guaranteed ticket to stardom. It was no different in Whoopi Goldberg's case. In 1991, the year following her Academy Award, she did scores of guest spots and specials on network and cable television. Among her TV appearances was *Blackbird Fly,* a half-hour drama about sexual abuse, which aired on the Learning Channel. She was the executive producer and star of a Nickelodeon program called *Tales from the Whoop: Hot Rod Brown, Class Clown,* for which she was nominated for a daytime Emmy Award.

Whoopi received another Emmy nomination for her guest appearance on the sitcom *A Different World,* in which she played a professor in whom a student with AIDS confides about her health. In August 1991, the first of Whoopi's three HBO projects was aired—a comedy special titled *Whoopi Goldberg: Chez Whoopi.*

Whoopi was also invited to be a judge at the prestigious Cannes Film Festival in France. Although she became embroiled in a controversy with black director Spike Lee, whose movie *Jungle Fever* was up for an award (she didn't vote for it), being selected as a judge was a true sign of the esteem in which other members of the film industry held her.

A few months before she received the Academy Award for her *Ghost* performance, Goldberg had signed a multimillion-dollar contract with Paramount Pictures. For a time, Paramount considered capitalizing on the success of her *Ghost* character and developing a follow-up that would trace the adventures of Oda Mae Brown, but the project never materialized. Instead, producers Herbert Ross and Aaron Spelling cast Whoopi as the veteran scriptwriter of a daytime soap opera in a comedy called *Soapdish.* Goldberg played Rose Schwartz, the confidante of the soap opera's neurotic lead actress, Celeste Talbert (Sally Field). It was an unusual role for Whoopi, who normally dressed casually and comfortably; she had the rare opportunity of dressing in expensive, elegant outfits, high heels, and fancy hairdos throughout the filming. *Soapdish* was not a big hit, but as usual, Whoopi received favorable reviews.

In February 1992, Whoopi Goldberg made history by being named the first female host of the annual Grammy Awards ceremony. She had clearly reached the pinnacle of her career. Her achievement seemed even greater because she now had her entire family close to her once again; her mother, brother, daughter, and grand-daughter now lived in the Los Angeles area.

That same year, Goldberg played a police detective in Robert Altman's film *The Player.* The movie was filled with cameo appearances by big-name stars, such as Cher, John Cusack, Jeff Goldblum, Anjelica Huston, Julia Roberts, Susan Sarandon, and Bruce Willis. But Whoopi's performance once again stood out. Altman remembers one particularly difficult scene that Whoopi Goldberg transformed with a few suggestions about what her character would be doing while speaking her lines. "And that's when I realized that she's so far above any tag that's hung on her that it borders on the supernatural," Altman enthused.

Whoopi's rise to fame was not over. In September 1991, Disney had offered her the starring role in a film called *Sister Act* after performer Bette Midler dropped out of the project. Whoopi played Deloris Van Cartier, a lounge singer who escapes from her mobster boyfriend when she witnesses him murdering one of his enemies. The police hide Deloris in a convent, where the raucous and irreverent singer, disguised as Sister Mary Clarence, transforms not only the nuns themselves but also the entire neighborhood in which they live.

Describing herself as "crabby" during the shooting of *Sister Act,* Whoopi says that she didn't enjoy the filming

A scene from the mildly successful 1991 comedy Soapdish, *starring Celeste Talbert (left), Sally Field (center), and Whoopi Goldberg.*

process this time around. She thought that the project had too many producers who spent too much time consulting studio executives. She was also very disappointed by the limited creative control she was allowed.

Despite these difficulties, *Sister Act,* which opened in May 1992, was a hugely popular movie. By the end of the year, it had earned nearly $140 million in North America. For her hilarious performance, Goldberg was nominated for a Golden Globe Award, and she won the People's Choice Award for Favorite Movie Actress of 1992.

Whoopi had no sooner completed filming on *Sister Act*

Disguised as Sister Mary Clarence, nightclub performer Deloris Van Cartier hopes for the best from the choir of nuns she has been training in the 1992 film Sister Act. *The movie was so successful that it generated a sequel,* Sister Act 2: Back in the Habit *(1993).*

than she began work on another movie called *Sarafina!* For Goldberg, *Sarafina!* represented a dramatic departure from her usual film projects. Set in South Africa, the story revolves around a teacher who is the mentor of a young black woman with dreams of Hollywood stardom.

Goldberg had considered turning down the part out of concern that she would be taking the role away from a South African actor. "But the people on that end [in South Africa] said I should come. I've always wanted to be in the eye of the storm, anyway, so I was both thrilled and nervous." Nevertheless, she insisted that her name appear after that of actress Leleti Khumalo in the film's credits. She did not want her own fame to overshadow the message of the film.

The film was shot on location in South Africa. Spending time in that country was a revelation for Goldberg. Apartheid laws, which not only sanctioned segregation but also discriminated politically and economically against blacks, had been abolished shortly before filming began. But Whoopi found that the emotional and mental scars of a segregated country were still in evidence. Even as a celebrity, she felt her freedom curtailed. "They have a shadow government down there and a secret police, and whew, those are rough guys," she recalled. "My passport disappeared from my hotel room while I was there." (It mysteriously reappeared later in a book that she had been reading.) Whoopi was dismayed by the stark contrast between the impoverished town of Soweto, with its squatters' shacks, and the lavish millionaire's home, complete with nine bathrooms, two swimming pools, a squash court, and servants' quarters, where she was invited as a party guest one evening.

Perhaps the most frightening aspect of her experience in South Africa was the need to be extremely cautious about security. Whoopi received several death threats from a local black group whose members were upset by the fact that an American, rather than a South African, had been offered an important role in the movie. With her usual candor, Goldberg managed to defuse the situation by agreeing to meet and speak with representatives from the group.

Again, Whoopi Goldberg received favorable reviews for her performance. For Whoopi, however, her experience emphasized how out of place she felt in Africa. Her

Whoopi Goldberg with Leleti Khumalo on the set of Sarafina! *Goldberg became the first African-American actress to shoot a film in South Africa, which was noted for its rigid, though now officially outlawed, policy of apartheid.*

time there only reinforced her feeling that she was an American through and through. "I'm not an African American," she said after *Sarafina!* was released. "I've met African folks. I've been in Africa, and I am . . . as American as Planet Hollywood and Mickie D's [McDonald's]."

After *Sarafina!*, Whoopi Goldberg was released from

her contract with Paramount Pictures. The company had undergone numerous executive changes and had not been able to find appropriate projects for her. Fortunately, however, Whoopi now had an entirely new project in the works. In the fall of 1991, a company called Genesis Entertainment had approached her about hosting her own late-night talk show.

Goldberg had already discussed this possibility with a few other firms, but Genesis Entertainment seemed willing to afford her a great deal of creative input. She agreed to host a half-hour show, for which each episode would be taped in advance. Goldberg was even able to hire Alexandrea to work for the program as a film-clip coordinator.

Whoopi wanted to do without some of the usual hallmarks of late-night talk shows, such as a "sidekick" personality, a house band, even a desk. She preferred a setting where she could talk with guests as though they were chatting in a private living room or den.

The advance publicity predicted moderate success for this offbeat talk show. "Industry buzz: Potential winner," the *New York Times* declared. "She's hot at the box office, her guest bookings are great. . . . Weaknesses: Shows will be taped far in advance, so forget topical edge. The host is inexperienced, and the audience may tune in for Whoopi-the-comedian, not Whoopi-the-interviewer."

The Whoopi Goldberg Show debuted on September 14, 1992, with Elizabeth Taylor as Whoopi's guest. During her first week, other guests included Ted Danson, Elton John, Robin Williams, and white supremacist Tom Metzger. But Whoopi's desire to be a congenial host seemed to keep her from asking stimulating questions. *Entertainment Weekly* gave her a "C+" rating, calling the show "the warmest, most buttery new talk show on television" but adding that "this normally hard-headed performer seems to have gone all soft and squishy." The *Hollywood Reporter* concurred: "Given the gregarious nature of its star, *The Whoopi Goldberg Show* is a surprisingly staid affair. The result is a show that displays little personality and only marginally more style."

Although Whoopi greatly enjoyed her stint as a talk-show host, the show's poor ratings led Genesis to cancel the show in May 1993. Despite its brief run, the show had run longer than a number of other talk shows that had been launched—and that failed—around the same time.

While working on the talk show, Whoopi had taken on a few other projects. One was a voice-over for a hyena character named Shenzi in the animated feature film *The Lion King.* In a lesser-known role, she provided another voice-over for Fantasy in *The Pagemaster.* In April of 1992, she had also begun filming *Made in America.* Whoopi played a woman who uses the services of a sperm bank to become pregnant after the death of her husband. Years later her daughter, Zora, becomes curious about the identity of her father. She eventually discovers that the man (played by Ted Danson) is white—a disreputable used-car salesman famous in the area for his lame TV commercials.

During the filming of *Made in America,* Goldberg became romantically involved with Danson, the star of the hit sitcom *Cheers,* who had been married for more than a decade to an environmental designer named Cassandra Coates. By September of 1992, rumors of the romance between Goldberg and Danson appeared in the national press, and a few months later the news hit the tabloids. In May 1993, Whoopi had begun shooting *Sister Act 2,* and Danson was a frequent visitor to the set. The following month, Danson's wife filed for divorce after 15 years of marriage.

Goldberg and Danson's relationship lasted only a few

Ted Danson with Whoopi Goldberg in a promotional shot for the 1993 movie Made in America. *The public relations disaster that occurred at the New York City Friars Club that year helped put an end to the couple's off-screen relationship and nearly derailed Goldberg's career.*

months beyond the end of his marriage. In October 1993, a public relations disaster involving the two actors would jeopardize not only their relationship but also Goldberg's career.

Goldberg had received the honor of being "roasted" at the prestigious New York City Friars Club, an organization that had been established around the turn of the century. The Friars Club had instituted a tradition of honoring notable personalities in the entertainment field with special annual luncheons or dinners. These events were called "roasts" because the honoree would be subject to good-natured (and sometimes bawdy) ribbing by his or her hosts. Among those who had been roasted were Humphrey Bogart, Lucille Ball, Bruce Willis, and Billy Crystal.

For Whoopi Goldberg's roast, Ted Danson had been named master of ceremonies. With about 40 other celebrities, including many black entertainers, Goldberg sat on a dais above an audience of more than 2,000 people, including members of the media. After having lunch and hearing a few speeches, the audience was completely unprepared for what happened next.

The curtains onstage opened to reveal Ted Danson, outfitted in a black tuxedo and a top hat. But that wasn't unusual. What horrified the audience was that Danson was in "blackface"—the style of stage makeup that white actors once used to play stereotypical blacks in the minstrel shows of the mid-19th century. Danson launched into a string of jokes that many members of the audience considered extremely offensive. Some were sexually explicit. Others were blatantly racist. After Danson told one joke about mulatto children, talk-show host Montel Williams, whose wife is white and whose child is biracial, stormed out of the auditorium. Throughout Danson's shocking performance, Goldberg laughed heartily—although almost no one joined her.

By the following day, the scandal had hit the papers. Williams had fired off an angry telegram to the chairman of the Friars Club, which read in part, "After the seven minutes that I stayed I was confused as to whether I was at a Friars event or at a rally for the KKK [Ku Klux Klan] and Aryan Nation." Most of those who attended the function sided with Williams. Spike Lee, in particular, railed against the couple. A few, such as comedian Jackie Mason, supported Goldberg and Danson. Mason complained that

Whoopi grandly welcomes the audience and TV viewers of the 68th annual Academy Awards ceremony in March 1996. Whoopi's first stint as host of the Academy Awards was in 1994, when she became the first black person and the first woman ever to emcee the event.

comedians "have to live in fear—we're not allowed to tell a joke anymore about certain subjects."

When Danson was branded a racist, Whoopi Goldberg leapt to his defense. She revealed that she had written much of his material and had hired the makeup artist to apply the blackface. The same week of the Friars Club roast, she and Danson appeared together on a Black Entertainment Network talk show, where she defended their actions. They'd deliberately chosen material they considered "so over-the-top that there would be no way . . . that anyone could construe [the act] as serious."

But they had gravely miscalculated. While Goldberg believed that the audience would realize that they were poking fun at outdated and unacceptable attitudes toward racial issues, her argument has failed to persuade many.

On November 5, 1993, a press release announced that Goldberg and Danson had gone their separate ways. In the aftermath of the Friars Club debacle, while working on a new movie called *Corrina, Corrina,* Whoopi met Lyle Trachtenberg, a union representative for the International Alliance of Theatrical Stage Employees. They were engaged in March 1994 and married the following October.

The marriage lasted less than two years. Whoopi filed for divorce on October 26, 1995. She later acknowledged that marrying so soon after her breakup with Danson had been a mistake. Following her divorce, she turned to her family more frequently for support and encouragement.

But the Johnson family, too, had had its share of trials during this period. Twenty-five years after Whoopi and her brother, Clyde, had last seen their father, Robert Johnson resurfaced. The pain Emma and her children had felt when they were abandoned by Johnson seemed to resurface with him, especially after they learned that he had incurable stomach cancer.

Johnson had apparently been a drug addict living hand-to-mouth for years before turning to religion in the 1980s and studying to become a minister at the New York Theological Seminary. He retired from his pulpit after six years and moved to Los Angeles, where he boasted to coworkers at his hospital job that he was Whoopi Goldberg's father. In 1992, Robert Johnson returned to his home state of South Carolina. There, he was diagnosed with cancer.

Until this point, Whoopi had had little, if any, contact

with her father. After her acting career took off and magazines and newspapers began to feature articles about her,
she still remained silent about him. On the rare occasions
when she spoke of him, she said that his desertion had hurt
so badly that she couldn't forgive him.

Whoopi did visit her father shortly before he underwent
surgery for his cancer. She even financed a Caribbean
cruise for him after his recovery. When he died on May
25, 1993, however, Whoopi could not bring herself to
attend the funeral as her brother Clyde did. Instead,
she sent a huge floral arrangement to the church where
services were held.

A triumphant Myrlie Evers (Goldberg), the wife of slain civil-rights leader Medgar Evers, in Ghosts of Mississippi. *Also appearing in the film were Darrell Evers (left), one of Myrlie and Medgar Evers's sons, who played himself; and Yolanda King (right), the daughter of Martin Luther King Jr., who played Evers's daughter, Reena.*

7

CELEBRITY AND ACTIVIST

THE CRITICISM WHOOPI GOLDBERG drew over the Friars Club fiasco continued after she accepted the role of a maid to a white man in the film *Corrina, Corrina*. The movie was a sweet-natured tale of a widower in the 1950s who hires a housekeeper to help care for his young daughter. Black groups declared that Goldberg was betraying her race by playing another subservient role. An angry Whoopi countered, "I say [we should] pay homage to these women who cleaned other people's houses to put their children through college and make them professors and the great men and women they became."

Nevertheless, the ad campaign for the film took great pains to avoid references to the romance that develops between the widower, Manny Singer (Ray Liotta) and his housekeeper (Goldberg). *Rolling Stone* acidly commented on this aspect. "Here's something new and unwelcome: a timid tear-jerker," it groused. Rating it a "C," *Entertainment Weekly* called it "*The Sound of Music* remade as an AT&T commercial."

In spite of the bad press and the disappointing reviews, Whoopi Goldberg still calls *Corrina, Corrina* one of her favorite projects. She explained her reasons:

Wilma the drive-in waitress (Patrika Darbo) and house-keeper Corrina (Whoopi Goldberg) coax Molly (Tina Majorino) into deciding what she wants to eat in a scene from the 1994 film Corrina, Corrina. *Responding to critics who faulted her for taking on another role that depicted a subservient black woman, Whoopi said that she intended to "pay homage to [the] women who cleaned other people's houses to put their children through college."*

Corrina looked good, dressed well, and was smart. She's articulate, a real person. She could be any of our mothers. . . . It's been the most romance I've had on-screen. This has less to do with my concept than with the powers-that-be's concept of what is sensual, beautiful, and acceptable. Those barriers are changing. There are more women out there that look like me than there were ten years ago.

In 1994, Whoopi rebounded from this difficult period when she was invited to host the 66th Annual Academy Awards ceremony—the first black and the first woman ever to do so. She was so popular that she was invited back two years later.

Whoopi Goldberg seemed to be coming into her own at last. Between 1995 and 1997, she was involved in 11 film projects. Although some, like *Eddie*, *Theodore Rex*, and *Bogus* (all released in 1996) were unsuccessful, others, such as *Boys on the Side* (1995), *Moonlight and Valentino* (1995), *Ghosts of Mississippi* (1996), and the HBO special *In the Gloaming* (1997) garnered favorable reviews.

Many film actresses have complained they receive fewer

roles as they near middle age. But Goldberg, now in her forties, still commands impressive paychecks for her work. Her two-picture deal with Disney in 1995 earned her $20 million, placing her among the highest-paid actors in Hollywood.

In February 1995 Goldberg received a lasting honor—she was invited to imprint her hands, feet, and trademark braids into the cement on the "walk of fame" at Hollywood's Mann's Chinese Theater. In 1997, she took another big step when, with the assistance of a ghostwriter, she wrote an anecdotal autobiography, *Book*. The same year she returned to theater, replacing actor Nathan Lane in *A Funny Thing Happened on the Way to the Forum*, then a huge hit on Broadway. She received rave reviews for her performance.

Like many celebrities, Whoopi sometimes resents the loss of privacy that comes with fame. "Every time I go anywhere or do anything," she once said, "it is always in the back of my mind whether or not I want to read about myself in the morning. I guess all that I am interested in reading about . . . is how I affected you in a film." Living with the knowledge that she is almost constantly under observation by the media has also put a strain on any relationships outside her circle of family and friends. Even dining out with an acquaintance can be misconstrued by tabloids as a budding romance. "I used to be able to go out with, you know, married friends of mine, go and have dinner or something. Can't do it anymore, you know?"

Whoopi has also felt stung by the criticism she's received from members of the black community concerning certain roles she has played, and wishes that she could have their support instead. She points out that she is a black woman who has managed to achieve success in an industry that has historically favored white actors of conventional physical beauty.

Goldberg remains one of Hollywood's biggest stars, and she is especially beloved by children. She has also remained very active in charity and fund-raising work— between 1994 and 1996, she raised money for 60 different

Holding a youngster, Whoopi participates in a 1995 Capitol Hill forum on proposed cuts in federal programs for children. A former welfare recipient, Goldberg is outspoken in her belief that the country's welfare system must be reformed.

charities. In addition to her continued involvement in the *Comic Relief* specials, which have raised more than $35 million for America's homeless, she has also contributed time and money to Elizabeth Taylor's AIDS Foundation and personally funds the medical bills and living expenses of several AIDS patients. In 1998, she published a book, *Breaking the Walls of Silence*, drawing attention to AIDS and women in prison.

Goldberg has also appeared with singer Gloria Estefan in a benefit for Florida hurricane victims. She campaigns actively to help young people fight drug abuse. In 1989, she was named Humanitarian of the Year by the Starlight Foundation, and she was honored in 1990 for contributions to the advancement of the status of women in the United

States. In 1991, Goldberg received the Norman Zarky Humanitarian Award, sponsored by Women in Film. In September 1997, Goldberg, Robin Williams, and Billy Crystal were recipients of Governors Awards by the Academy of Television Arts and Sciences for their work in *Comic Relief*. Whoopi Goldberg's commitment to such causes is best summed up by her reply when asked about her involvement in the first *Comic Relief* benefit: "It's not somebody else's problem," she responded.

Goldberg's first stint as a producer began with a new version of the *Hollywood Squares* TV game show, which debuted in September 1998. She also plans to star in and produce a new TV series for CBS called *Harlem*, and she is working on producing a stage version of the 1967 Julie Andrews movie *Thoroughly Modern Millie*. She also appeared in film adaptations of two bestselling novels, Terry McMillan's *How Stella Got Her Groove Back* (1998) and Jacqueline Mitchard's *The Deep End of the Ocean* (1999).

Whatever her upcoming projects may be, the woman who grew up in the Chelsea projects of New York and dreamed of becoming a movie star seems determined to remain in the limelight. She acknowledges that she would not be where she is without the love and support of her family—especially her mother and brother—and the courage of role models who remained fixed on their goals. "I was raised to believe that I could become part of the fabric of this country no matter what it was I wanted to do, you know? . . . And Mom gave [this faith] to me, President Kennedy gave it to me, my big brother gave it to me, Harry Belafonte gave it to me—people who went out and *did* gave it to me."

Today, Whoopi says, she is one of the luckiest people in the world: "I do what I want. I look the way I want. . . . I have a healthy kid, healthy grandkids. My mom is still with me, and I've got a great brother and a man in my life [actor Frank Langella] and a cat who loves me." For Whoopi Goldberg, it seems life can't get any better.

CHRONOLOGY

1955   Born Caryn Johnson on November 13 in New York City

1963   Begins acting with the Helena Rubinstein Performing Arts Workshops at the Hudson Guild

1969   Graduates from St. Columba's School and enters Washington Irving High School

1972   Drops out of high school; checks into Horizon House for drug rehabilitation; marries her drug counselor

1973   Gives birth to daughter, Alexandrea

1974   Divorces husband; moves to San Diego, California, with her daughter

1976   Joins San Diego Repertory Theater

1979   Moves to Berkeley and joins Blake Street Hawkeyes

1983   Gains recognition in New York City with *The Spook Show*

1984   *Whoopi Goldberg* opens on Broadway

1985   Receives Golden Globe Award for Best Performance by an Actress, Academy Award nomination for Best Actress, and NAACP Image Award for Best Actress in a Motion Picture for *The Color Purple;* wins Grammy Award for Best Comedy Recording for *Whoopi Goldberg: Direct from Broadway*

1986   Stars in *Jumpin' Jack Flash;* cohosts the first *Comic Relief* benefit for the homeless with Robin Williams and Billy Crystal; receives Emmy Award nomination for Best Guest Performer in a Dramatic Series for *Moonlighting*

1987   Featured in *Burglar* and *Fatal Beauty*

1988   Nominated for an American Comedy Award as Funniest Female Performer in a TV Special for "Carol, Carl, Whoopi, and Robin"; stars in *Clara's Heart;* receives Ace Award nomination for HBO's *Whoopi Goldberg's Fontaine: Why Am I Straight?*

1990   Costars with Sissy Spacek in *The Long Walk Home;* testifies before a U.S. Senate committee on behalf of the homeless; appears in the film *Ghost*

1991   Wins Academy, Golden Globe, British Academy, NAACP Image, and American Comedy Awards for Best Supporting Actress for *Ghost*; writes children's book, *Alice;* named Entertainer of the Year by NAACP Image Awards

1992   Stars in *Sister Act* and the musical drama *Sarafina!;* appears in *The Player;* hosts a late-night talk show; receives Emmy for *Star Trek: The Next Generation;* wins Ace Award for *Comic Relief V;* becomes first female host of the Grammy Awards

1993   Costars with Ted Danson in *Made in America;* becomes one of Hollywood's highest-paid performers with the release of *Sister Act 2: Back in the Habit;* receives two People's Choice Awards, an NAACP Image Award, and American Comedy Award for *Sister Act*

1994   Hosts the 66th Annual Academy Awards; appears in feature films *Star Trek: Generations; Corrina, Corrina;* and *The Lion King* (as the voice of the animated character Shenzi)

1995   Costars in *Boys on the Side, Moonlight and Valentino;* named to the Walk of Fame at Hollywood's Mann's Chinese Theater

1996   Hosts the 68th Annual Academy Awards; stars in *Ghosts of Mississippi;* receives honorary doctorate from Brandeis University

1997   Appears in the Broadway revival of *A Funny Thing Happened on the Way to the Forum;* costars in the HBO film *In the Gloaming; Book* is published; appears in the TV version of Rodgers & Hammerstein's *Cinderella;* shares with Billy Crystal and Robin Williams the Governors Award from the Academy of Television Arts & Sciences for *Comic Relief* fund-raising specials

1998   Is honored for her 20-year career in film, stage, and television at the 24th Annual People's Choice Awards; appears in the film adaptation of *How Stella Got Her Groove Back;* becomes a regular on the TV game show *Hollywood Squares*

1999   Appears in the film adaptation of *The Deep End of the Ocean*

The award-winning actress leaves an imprint of her braids in the Walk of Fame at Mann's Chinese Theater in Hollywood, 1995.

FILMOGRAPHY

Selected Theater, Film, and Television Appearances

FILM

The Color Purple (1985)
Jumpin' Jack Flash (1986)
Burglar (1987)
Fatal Beauty (1987)
The Telephone (1988)
Clara's Heart (1988)
Beverly Hills Brats (cameo, 1989)
Ghost (1990)
Homer and Eddie (1990)
The Long Walk Home (1990)
House Party 2 (cameo, 1991)
Soapdish (1991)
The Player (1992)
Sister Act (1992)
Wisecracks (1992)
The Magical World of Chuck Jones (interviewee, 1992)
Sarafina! (1992)
Made in America (1993)
National Lampoon's Loaded Weapon I (cameo, 1993)
Sister Act 2: Back in the Habit (1993)
Naked in New York (1994)
The Lion King (voice only, 1994)
The Little Rascals (cameo, 1994)
Corinna, Corinna (1994)
Star Trek: Generations (1994)
The Pagemaster (voice only, 1994)
Liberation (co-narrator, 1994)
Boys on the Side (1995)
Moonlight and Valentino (1995)
Eddie (1996)
Theodore Rex (1996)
Tales from the Crypt Presents: Bordello of Blood (cameo, 1996)
Bogus (1996)

The Associate (1996)
Ghosts of Mississippi (1996)
In and Out (cameo, 1997)
Burn Hollywood Burn (An Alan Smithee Film) (1998)
State and Maine (1998)
How Stella Got Her Groove Back (1998)
The Deep End of the Ocean (1999)

TELEVISION

Whoopi Goldberg: Direct from Broadway (HBO, 1985)
A Carol Burnett Special: Carol, Carl, Whoopi, & Robin (1986)
Comic Relief HBO Specials (cohost, 1986–99)
Moonlighting (guest appearance, 1986)
Star Trek: The Next Generation (1987–94)
Captain EO: Backstage (host, 1987)
A Different World (guest appearance, 1987)
Dolly (guest appearance, 1987)
Scared Straight: Ten Years Later (host, 1987)
The Making of Disney's Captain EO (host, 1988)
Freedomfest: Nelson Mandela's 70th Birthday Celebration (cohost, 1988)
CBS Schoolbreak Special: "My Past Is My Own" (1989)
Kiss Shot (CBS movie, 1989)
Tales from the Crypt (guest appearance, 1989)
A Laugh, A Tear (host, coproducer, 1990)
Whoopi Goldberg and Billy Connolly in Performance (costar, executive producer, 1990)
That's What Friends Are For (cohost, 1990)
Happy Birthday, Bugs! 50 Looney Years (1990)
The 15th Annual Circus of the Stars (co-ringmaster, 1990)
Bagdad Café (1990–91)
Captain Planet and the Planeteers (voice only, 1990–93)
Tales from the Whoop: Hot Rod Brown, Class Clown (star, executive producer, 1991)
Ray Charles: 50 Years in Music, Uh-Huh! (host, 1991)
Whoopi Goldberg: Chez Whoopi (host, 1991)
The Whoopi Goldberg Show (1992–93)
The 34th Annual Grammy Awards (host, 1992)
Hurricane Relief (host, 1992)

A Gala for the President at Ford's Theater (host, 1993)
The 64th Annual Academy Awards (host, 1994)
Voodoo Lounge (music video, 1994)
The Celluloid Closet (HBO movie, 1995)
The Sunshine Boys (guest appearance, 1995)
The Muppets Tonight! (guest appearance, 1996)
The 68th Annual Academy Awards (host, 1996)
Rodgers & Hammerstein's Cinderella (1997)
Destination Anywhere (music video, 1997)
In the Gloaming (HBO movie, 1997)
Hollywood Squares (1998)

THEATER

Whoopi Goldberg (1984)
A Funny Thing Happened on the Way to the Forum (1997)
Thoroughly Modern Millie (1999)

BIBLIOGRAPHY

Adams, Mary Agnes. *Whoopi Goldberg: From Street to Stardom.* New York: Dillon Press, 1993.

Blue, Rose, and Corinne J. Naden. *Whoopi Goldberg.* New York: Chelsea House Publishers, 1995.

Bogle, Donald. *Blacks in American Films and Television.* New York: Garland Publishing, 1988.

Brode, Douglas. *The Films of Stephen Spielberg.* Secaucus, NJ: Citadel Press, 1995.

Goldberg, Whoopi. *Book.* New York: Rob Weisbach Books, 1997.

Katz, Sandor. *Whoopi Goldberg: Performer with a Heart.* Philadelphia: Chelsea House Publishers, 1997.

Parish, James Robert. *Whoopi Goldberg: Her Journey from Poverty to Mega-Stardom.* Secaucus, NJ: Birch Lane Press, 1997.

Walker, Alice. *The Color Purple.* New York: Pocket Books, 1982.

APPENDIX

ORGANIZATIONS THAT HELP PREGNANT TEENS AND TEEN PARENTS

Advocates for Youth
1025 Vermont Avenue, N.W.
Suite 200
Washington, DC 20005
202-347-5700
info@advocatesforyouth.org
http://www.advocatesforyouth.org/

Alan Guttmacher Institute
120 Wall Street
New York, NY 10005
212-248-1111
info@agi-usa.org
http://www.agi-usa.org

Association of Maternal and Child Health Programs
1220 19th Street, N.W.
Suite 801
Washington, DC 20036
202-775-0436
info@amchp.org
http://www.amchp1.org

Baby Think It Over Program
2709 Mondovi Road
Eau Claire, WI 54701
800-830-1416
715-830-2040
information@btio.com
http://btio.com/

Child Welfare League of America
440 First Street, N.W., 3rd Floor
Washington, DC 20001-2085
202-638-2952
http://www.arhp.org/narhp/orgsteens.html

FDA Teen Scene
http://www.fda.gov/opacom/7teens/html

Go Ask Alice!
(interactive question-and-answer service)
http://www.goaskalice.columbia.edu/about.html

Planned Parenthood Federation of America
810 Seventh Avenue
New York, NY 10019
212-541-7800
communications@ppfa.org
http://www.plannedparenthood.org

Sex Etc. (teen-produced website)
http://www.rci.rutgers.edu/~sxetc/

Sexuality Information and Education Council of the United States
130 West 42nd Street, Suite 350
New York, NY 10036-7802
212-819-9770
siecus@siecus.org
http://www.siecus.org/

Teen Line (Service of Iowa Dept. of Public Health)
800-443-8336
http://www.exnet.iastate.edu/pages/cahotlines/teenline

ORGANIZATIONS THAT HELP PEOPLE
WITH ALCOHOL AND OTHER DRUG ABUSE PROBLEMS

**Alateen, Al-Anon Family Group
Headquarters, Inc.**
1600 Corporate Landing Parkway
Virginia Beach, VA 23454-5617
757-563-1600

American Council for Drug Education
164 West 74th Street
New York, NY 10023
800-488-DRUG
http://www.acde.org/default.cfm

Cocaine Anonymous
World Service Office
3740 Overland Avenue, Suite G
Los Angeles, CA 90034
800-347-8998
213-559-5833

Families Anonymous
P.O. Box 528
Van Nuys, CA 91408
818-989-7841

Narcotics Anonymous
World Service Office
P.O. Box 9999
Van Nuys, CA 91409
818-780-3951

National Center for Tobacco-Free Kids
1707 L Street, N..W., Suite 800
Washington, DC 20036
202-296-5469
800-284-KIDS

**National Clearinghouse
for Alcohol and Drug Information
(NCADI)/Center for Substance Abuse
Prevention (CSAP)**
P.O. Box 2345
Rockville, MD 20847-2345
800-SAY-NOTO
http://www.health.org

National Family Partnership
(c/o Greenville Family Partnership)
P.O. Box 10203
617 East McBee Avenue
Greenville, SC 29601
864-467-4009

National Institute on Drug Abuse (NIDA)
5600 Fishers Lane, Room 10A03
Rockville, MD 20857
301-443-4577
http://www.nida.nih.gov/

**Office of National Drug Control Policy
(ONDCP)**
Washington, DC 20503
E-mail: ondcp@ncjrs.org
http://www.whitehousedrugpolicy.gov/

**Parents' Resource Institute
for Drug Education (PRIDE)**
50 Hurt Plaza, Suite 210
Atlanta, GA 30303
770-458-9900
800-853-7867
http://www.prideusa.org/

Partnership for a Drug-Free America
http://www.drugfreeamerica.org/

ORGANIZATIONS THAT
HELP PEOPLE WITH DYSLEXIA

Davis Dyslexia Association International
1601 Old Bayshore Highway
Suite 245
Burlingame, CA 94010
650-692-8995
ddai@dyslexia.com
http://www.dyslexia.com/

Dyslexia Association of America/
Michigan Dyslexia Institute, Inc.
532 East Shiawassee Street
Lansing, MI 48912
517-485-4000
800-832-3535
http://cybersytes.com/mdi/mdi.htm

International Dyslexia Association
8600 LaSalle Road
Chester Building, Suite 382
Baltimore, MD 21286-2044
410-296-0232
http://www.interdys.org/

INDEX

PICTURE CREDITS

Ann Graham Gaines, the author of several books for young adults, is a freelance writer who lives in Gonzales, Texas.

James Scott Brady serves on the board of trustees with the Center to Prevent Handgun Violence and is the Vice Chairman of the Brain Injury Foundation. Mr. Brady served as Assistant to the President and White House Press Secretary under President Ronald Reagan. He was severely injured in an assassination attempt on the president, but remained the White House Press Secretary until the end of the administration. Since leaving the White House, Mr. Brady has lobbied for stronger gun laws. In November 1993, President Bill Clinton signed the Brady Bill, a national law requiring a waiting period on handgun purchases and a background check on buyers.